COPYRIGHT FOR LIBRARIANS

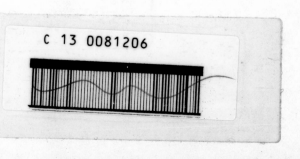

COPYRIGHT FOR LIBRARIANS

by L. J. Taylor

Tamarisk Books

Hastings, 1980

British Library Cataloguing in Publication data:

Taylor, Laurence John
 Copyright for librarians.
 1. Copyright – Great Britain
 I. Title
 346'.41'0482   KD1289

ISBN 0–907221–00–9

Copyright © 1980 by Laurence John Taylor

First published 1980, by Tamarisk Books, West Hill Cottage, Exmouth Place, Hastings, East Sussex TN34 3JA

Printed by W. A. Guy & Jones Ltd., High Street, Hastings, East Sussex, TN34 3HL

in Intertype Plantin 8 and 10 pt.

Contents

Preface and Acknowledgements

This book is written for practising librarians (though I hope students will also find it interesting), and has two purposes. The first is to set out more fully than I believe has been done anywhere else the law of copyright as it currently applies to the work of librarians. The second is to contribute to the discussion on possible changes to copyright law in the U.K., as a consequence of the Whitford report of 1977.

The basic question for librarians: 'Can I copy it?' on which I offer a simplified algorithm, serves as an introduction to a close study of the relevant sections of the Copyright Act 1956, and the Libraries Regulations of 1957, followed by a chapter of more detailed questions and answers. I have tried to envisage situations in which a librarian finds himself unsure about copyright law concerning written texts. The answers are discursive but do try to offer a positive recommendation for action in each case. Chapter 7, on microforms and audio visual materials, also deals with interpretations of the present law, but in the context of the proposed changes.

The current debate on possible changes to the law is the focus of chapter 5 in which the Whitford report and the submissions that preceded it and the responses that followed are considered, and chapter 6, in which the specific issue of the influence of photocopying on journal sales is discussed. There is also a section of chapter 7 on implications for computers, and other general chapters on the recent history of copyright.

The chapter on overseas copyright is included to provide a context for the current debate, since it seems likely that the example of the United States, and the pressures from the EEC will both play important parts in influencing the outcome. The final chapter offers a theoretical basis for the arguments that must still be to come.

I must make it abundantly clear that the interpretations of the law and opinions on what actions it permits or prohibits are not those of a qualified lawyer. They are my own, based on my experience of dealing with copyright enquiries as the Library Association's Information Officer over a period of ten years, and on fairly wide reading. Should any librarian become involved in legal actions, he should always consult a professional adviser.

The reasons for my venturing into print to give opinions on the law are:

I suspect a certain amount of law breaking is done by librarians and their users, unaware of the law;

the legal texts offer little or no guidance on library matters because there has been no case law;

the Act and Regulations are couched in language that is difficult to apply to actual circumstances, and in places appears to be contradictory;

previous published commentary on the law by librarians is in scattered places, and some of it, I feel, is unreliable.

I have benefited considerably from my membership of the Library Association's Sub-committee on Copyright over the last seven years — its deliberations have helped me to form my own views more clearly. To Geoffrey Crabb of the Council for Educational Technology and to Frank Graham, Chairman of the LA's Sub-committee on Copyright, I am especially grateful, as they have read this book in draft, and offered me many suggestions and corrections of detail, which I have been happy to incorporate. They are in no way responsible, of course, for any shortcomings that remain. I have also been greatly assisted by the facilities of the Library Association Library, which have led me to my chief debt — the multitude of writers on copyright. Those I have used are listed in the bibliography, and from time to time are cited in the text. My apologies are offered to any author whose views I may unwittingly have adopted without attribution.

L. J. Taylor
June 1980

Can I copy it? - a brief algorithm

001 Is a substantial part to be copied? (see 208, 250-3). If it is not the copy may be made. If it is go to 002.

002 Is it published or unpublished? (see 119, 210). If published, is it in copyright (see 213). If in copyright, go to 003, if not it may be copied. If it is not published go to 043.

003 Is it a literary, dramatic, musical or artistic work? in microform (go to 040), a sound recording (see 730), or a film (see 736). If literary, dramatic or musical, go to 004, if artistic go to 035, if a sound recording go to 041, if a film or videotape go to 042.

004 It is a literary, dramatic or musical work. Are you acting as an individual or as a librarian? If as a librarian go to 005. If as an individual go to 027.

005 You are acting as a librarian. Is your library one of those prescribed under the Libraries Regulations (see 106, 237-8). If so go to 006, if not go to 020.

006 Your library is prescribed. Is the item a periodical (see 247) or another publication? If a periodical go to 007, if another publication go to 013.

007 The item is a periodical. Are you intending to take a single copy or more than one? If a single copy go to 008, if more than one, note that this is not permitted.

008 A single copy is wanted. Is one article wanted or more? (see 243). If one article or a part of one is wanted go to 009. If more than one note that this is not permitted, but see 244.

009 A single article is wanted. Do you wish to make this copy for stock, for a library user, or in response to another library's request? If for stock, note this is not permitted, but see 272-5. If for a library user, go to 010, if for another library go to 011.

010 The copy is for a library user. Has a declaration been properly completed (see 107, 262-3), and has payment been made (see 257-60)? If so the copy may be made, if neither or only one condition is fulfilled the copy may not be made.

011 The copy is for another library. Is the library one of those prescribed? (see 106, 237-8). If so go to 012. If not the copy is not permitted.

012 The requesting library is one of those prescribed. The copy may be made if the conditions are fulfilled (see 108-9).

013 The item is not a periodical publication. If it is a microform go to 040, if an artistic work go to 035, if a sound recording go to 041, if a film go to 042, if a printed publication go to 014.

014 The item is a printed publication. Is the quantity to be copied within the guidelines of *Photocopying and the law?* (see 405-8), or if a musical work, within the guidelines of *Copying music?* (see 540-1). If so the copy may be made provided the conditions are fulfilled (see 107, 262-3). If not, has the copyright owner given permission? If so the copy may be made, if not go to 015.

015 The copyright owner has not given permission. Have you made reasonable enquiry (see 109, 121) to discover the name and address of the copyright owner? If not this must be done and permission obtained; if you have made reasonable enquiry, go to 016.

016 You have failed after reasonable enquiry to locate the copyright owner. Is the copy to be made for stock, for a library user, or for another library? If for stock, this is not permitted, but see 272-5. If for a library user go to 017, if for another library, go to 018.

017 The copy is for a library user. Is the copy a reasonable part (see 250-3) and has a declaration been completed and payment been made (see 107, 262-3; 257-60). If so the copy may be made, if only one or two of these conditions are fulfilled the copy may not be made.

018 The copy is for another library. Is the library one of those prescribed? (see 106, 237-8)? If not the copy may not be made, if it is, go to 019.

019 The copy is for a prescribed library. If the conditions are fulfilled (see 108-9), the copy may be made, if not the copy is not permitted.

020 Your library is not prescribed, and you may not copy for library users under the Libraries Regulations. Is the copy for another prescribed library? If so go to 026, if not go to 021.

021 The copy is not for another, prescribed, library. Is the copy for stock, or for a library user? If for stock, note that this not permitted, but see 272-5; if for a library user, go to 022.

022 The copy is for a library user. Is the copy a single copy of a periodical article (see 243, 247-9)? If so, it may be made under the protection of *Photocopying and the law* (see 305-8), if not go to 023.

023 Is the copy a single copy of a part of another publication, not extending beyond the limits given in *Photocopying and the law* (see 305-8), or if a musical work, not beyond the guidelines of *Copying music*? If it is not, the copy may not be made, if it is, go to 024.

024 The copy is within the guidelines of *Photocopying and the law* or *Copying music*. Does the item to be copied bear a warning against unauthorised copying? If it does, the copy should not be made. If it does not the copy can probably be made safely. (see 288).

025 The copy is for another library. Is the receiving library a prescribed library (see 106, 237-8)? If not the copy may not be made. If it is go to 026.

026 The copy is for a prescribed library. Is the library making the copy freely open to the public (see 106)? If the conditions are complied with (see 108-9), the copy may be made.

027 You are acting not as a librarian, but as an individual. If you are using a library to obtain your copies, what may be copied for you is set out in 004 and connected paragraphs. If you are copying for yourself go to 028.

028 You are copying for yourself. Is the purpose of the copying research or private study? If it is go to 029, if not go to 030.

029 The copy is for research or private study. Can it be described as fair dealing (see 228)? If so the copy may be made, if not it is not permitted.

030 The copy is not for purposes of research or private study. Is it for purposes of criticism or review? If it is go to 031, if not go to 032.

031 The copy is for purposes of criticism or review. Can it be described as fair dealing (see 228-9)? If so the copy may be made, if not, it is not permitted.

032 The copy is not for purposes of criticism or review. Is it for purposes of reporting current events? If it is go to 033, if not go to 034.

033 The copy is for reporting current events. Can it be described as fair dealing? (see 228-9) If so the copy may be made, if not, go to 034.

034 The copy is not for reporting current events. Other exceptions from protection are dealt with in Section 6 of the Copyright Act (see 114), but they are unlikely to apply to librarians or their users.

035 It is an artistic work. Does it explain or illustrate a literary or dramatic work which is being copied? If so it counts as part of that work (go to 004 and connected sections), if not go to 036.

036 It is a separate artistic work. Is the copy justifiable as fair dealing for purposes of research or private study, or for purposes of criticism or review? If so the copy may be made, if not go to 037.

037 The copy is not justifiable as fair dealing. Is the work in two dimensions or three? If in two dimensions go to 039, if in three go to 038.

038 The work is in three dimensions. Is it permanently sited in a public place or in a building open to the public? If it is a two dimensional copy may be made. If not the copy is not permitted.

039 The artistic work is in two dimensions. Is the copying to take the form of a film or television broadcast, in which the work's representation is only incidental to the rest of the film or broadcast? If so, the copy may be made, if neither or only one condition applies the copy may not be made.

040 The work is in microform. Some microforms are protected as literary, dramatic or musical works, some may be protected as artistic works. For discussion of this area see 701-10.

041 The work is a sound recording. Copying onto or from sound recordings is a complicated matter, as several rights are frequently involved. (e.g. music, words, and performers' rights). For discussion of this area see 730-5.

042 The work is a film or videotape. Copying onto or from film or videotape is a complicated matter, involving several rights. For a discussion of this area see 736-42.

043 The work is unpublished. Is it in a library or other similar institution and generally accessible to the public? (see 103, 215-16). If it is go to 044, if not the copy may not be made.

044 The work is in a publicly open library or similar institution. Has more than fifty years elapsed since the end of the year in which the author died, and has more than 100 years elapsed since the work was made? If both conditions apply, go to 045. If neither or only one condition applies the copy is not permitted.

045 Both prescribed conditions apply to the unpublished work in a library or similar institution. Is the copy for purposes of research or private study, or with a view to publication? If for research or private study, the copy may be made. If for publication, see 104, 217, for further conditions.

1
The Law as it stands

101   The aim of this chapter is to draw attention to those parts of the law
as it is at present, that are of concern to the librarian, to summarise
or paraphrase them, but not to offer specific interpretations: that is
the subject of chapter 2. This paragraph gives a bald simplification
of copyright: for detailed discussion of the general nature of copyright,
restricted acts, qualified persons, and assignments and licences, the
reader is referred to the Copyright Act itself, and to legal commentaries
on it. Copyright in the U.K. is the right to do certain acts in relation
to certain works, and is available to certain categories of person. The
works protected are literary, dramatic, musical and artistic (described
as 'original'), and sound recordings, cinematograph films, television
and sound broadcasts, and published editions of works. In relation to
literary, dramatic and musical works, the acts restricted by copyright
are reproducing the work in a material form, publishing it, performing
it in public, broadcasting or relaying it over a diffusion service, and
adapting it. Adaptation includes translation. Artistic works are
restricted from being reproduced, published or included in television
or diffusion broadcasts. Restricted acts in sound recordings are making
a further recording of it, playing it in public, or broadcasting it. Films
may not be copied, played in public (sound or vision tracks), broadcast or diffused. Television and sound broadcasts may not be copied
except for private purposes, played in public, or re-broadcast.
Published editions are protected against photographic or similar
reproductions of the typographic arrangement of the edition. The
holder of copyright is the first author or creator of the work, provided
he or she is a qualified person, which generally means a British or
British protected subject. (International conventions protect the copyrights of other nationals in this country). Copyright may be assigned
or licensed to another in whole or in part, as though it were a
moveable property. But there are various exceptions to the exclusivity
of copyright.

Exceptions for libraries and archives

102   As there is one section specifically devoted to libraries and archives,

I consider that first, even though I shall have something to say about an earlier Section later: logical arrangement of Sections in the 1956 Act is not its strong feature, so little harm will be done by this. Section 7, given the shoulder note 'Special exceptions as respects libraries and archives' has 10 sub-sections and occupies more than three full pages of the Act. Much of the detail is repeated or rephrased in the 1957 Regulations, so only brief attention is needed for much of it here, since I shall be looking at the Regulations more closely later (205-11). Sub-section 1 refers to the making of single copies of periodicals by prescribed libraries and the issuing of regulations by the Board of Trade, setting out conditions for making these copies. Sub-section 2 instructs the Board of Trade to include five conditions in their regulations, relating to the status of the library, the research or private study purposes in making the copies, limiting copies to one per person, and to one article per publication, and to requiring payment for the copy. Sub-section 3 allows prescribed libraries to make copies of parts of works provided the libraries cannot discover the identity of the copyright owner. Sub-section 4 repeats the conditions in 2 and adds that only a 'reasonable' amount of a work may be copied. Sub-section 5 sets out conditions for one library supplying another with copies, even complete works.

Sub-section 6

103 This is the first not to be repeated or amplified in the Regulations, and requires closer attention. It provides for reproduction for research or private study or for publication of unpublished works held in libraries, museums or other institutions that are open to public inspection. The conditions for this permission are first that the author must have died at such a time that any of his published works would be out of copyright (i.e. fifty years after the end of the year in which he died) and secondly that one hundred years must have elapsed since the work was made. There is also the proviso that this permission is subject to the rules and regulations of the institution in question.

Sub-section 7

104 This extends the meaning of Sub-section 6 concerning the publication of unpublished works held in publicly open institutions. Sub-section 6 states how copies may be made either for research or private study, or 'with a view to publication'. The conditions for actually completing that publication are laid down here. These state that anyone proposing a new publication incorporating part or all of an unpublished work described in Sub-section 6 must first issue a notice of such intent, to be prescribed by the Board of Trade, and ensure that the identity of no copyright owner of the unpublished work is known to the publisher immediately prior to publication. The Board of Trade Regulation in this instance is Copyright (Notice of Publication)

Regulations, 1957 (S.I. 1957 No. 865). It calls for notice to publish to be put into a daily or Sunday newspaper with a national circulation (see 217). Sub-section 8 extends the protection of Sub-section 7 to the broadcasting, diffusion, public performance or recording of the work. Sub-section 9 explains that references to a work or part of a work should include accompanying artistic explanatory or illustrative works. In other words, where an act of copying a text or part of a text is not a copyright infringement, neither is the act of copying any illustrations that go with it. Sub-section 10 states that the term article, used in the Section refers to an item of any description.

The Regulations

105 The document's full title is The Copyright (Libraries) Regulations, 1957 (S.I. 1957 No. 868), and it came into effect on 1st June 1957. Its preamble refers to its authority in Section 7 and sub-section (4) of Section 15 of the Copyright Act 1956. (Section 15 relates to copyright in typographical arrangement, and is to be discussed later (116).)

Prescribed libraries

106 Sections 1-3 of the Regulations set out the nature of prescribed libraries that are permitted to take advantage of the Regulations to the full. These are described in Schedule 1. They comprise the legal deposit libraries, libraries in education (schools, universities, university colleges, or any further education establishment); public libraries; parliamentary and government department libraries; and libraries that are 'conducted for, or administered by an establishment or organisation conducted for, the purpose of facilitating or encouraging the study of all or any of the following:- religion, philosophy, science (including any natural or social science), technology, medicine, history, literature, languages, education, bibliography, fine arts, music or law'. A second schedule, simply reading 'Any library which makes works in its custody available to the public free of charge' is set out for purposes of sub-section 5 of the Regulations (libraries copying for other libraries, see below).
Sub-section 3 confirms that libraries permitted to copy under Section 7 of the Act are not restricted from so doing by the copyright in typographical arrangement.

Sub-section 4

107 This sets out the prescribed conditions for library copying. These are four:

Declaration
    No copy under these Regulations may be made unless the person receiving it has delivered a declaration to the librarian substantially

in the specified form. The declaration, a form for which is Schedule 3 of the Regulations, makes three statements

(a) that the copy is required for research or private study;

(b) that the recipient has not previously been supplied with the *same* item by *any* librarian;

(c) that the recipient will not use the copy except for research or private study.

A note adds that the signature on the declaration must be that of the individual making the request. It must not be stamped or typewritten and it may not be that of an agent for the requester.

Articles in periodicals

No copy extending to more than one article in any one publication may be made in the case of periodicals copying.

Reasonable proportion

No copy of more than a 'reasonable proportion' of a work may be made in the case of items that are not periodical articles.

Payment

The recipient of a copy must pay the library a sum not less than the cost of making it, which should include a contribution to the library's general expenses.

Sub-section 5

108 This deals with making copies for libraries by other libraries, and three specific conditions are laid down:

(a) copies may not be supplied if the same item has been supplied before unless the supplying librarian is satisfied that any previous copy has been lost, destroyed or damaged;

(b) libraries must pay for copies received in the same way as individuals;

(c) libraries may not supply copies to libraries that are established or conducted for profit.

Sub-section 6

109 This removes much of the protection of sub-section 5 by stipulating that libraries may not supply copies of complete works or parts of works to other libraries if they know or could by reasonable enquiry discover the name and address of the copyright holder.

Sub-section 7

110 This protects libraries operating under these Regulations from breach of copyright in typographical arrangement (Section 15 of the Act). The librarian is not under an obligation to obtain permission from the copyright owner in such cases when making a copy.

Sub-sections 8 and 9

111 These deal with interpretation, indicating the 1956 Copyright Act as being the Act referred to in the Regulations, and 'work' as meaning a published literary, dramatic or musical work. The 1889 Interpretation Act is to apply to interpreting these Regulations. The final sub-section 10 gives the citation of the Regulations as the 'Copyright (Libraries) Regulations 1957', and the date of commencement as 1st June 1957.

Fair dealing

112 Under the shoulder note 'General exceptions from protection of literary, dramatic and musical works' Section 6 of the 1956 Act is found. This is generally known as the 'fair dealing clause', though only the first three of its 10 sub-sections refer to fair dealing as such, and only the first sub-section is at all frequently invoked by librarians. The first three sub-sections state that no fair dealing with literary, dramatic and musical works is an infringement if:

(1) it is for the purpose of research or private study
(2) it is for the purposes of criticism or review (provided acknowledgement is made)
(3) it is for the purpose of reporting current events (provided acknowledgement of any printed source is made)

113 The third of these may occasionally be applicable in library situations, as when current awareness bulletins are prepared, but the principal interest in the Section as a whole for librarians is in the first sub-section. It is, however, debatable whether library copying is offered any protection by it, and this point will be considered in chapter 2 (228-36).

114 The remaining sub-sections of Section 6 of the Act have even less relevance to library matters. They offer the following exceptions from infringement:

(4) reproduction for judicial proceedings
(5) recitation in public (but not for broadcasting)
(6) inclusion of passages in collections for schools (with detailed provisos)
(7) making of temporary copies for purposes of authorised broadcasting
(8) a similar exception to (7) covering licensed adaptations
(9) a similar exception for diffusion services
(10) a definition of sufficient acknowledgement, as required in making copies under sub-sections (2), (3), (5), (6). It is defined as identifying a work by its title and author.

Other exceptions

115   Section 8 of the Act concerns protection in making gramophone records of musical works and literary works as integral parts of musical works. The main purpose of the section is to allow for making records upon payment of a statutory royalty, which the Act fixes at $6\frac{1}{4}\%$ of the retail selling price, but allows the Board of Trade to vary by Statutory Order. Section 9 gives various protections to copying artistic works. These include fair dealing for research or private study, or criticism or review in sub-sections (1) and (2). Representations in two dimensions of objects in three dimensions are also not infringements, if the artistic work is permanently sited in a public place or on public premises, or if the representation is made for reporting purposes. Publication of representations made under these conditions is also permitted. Reproductions for judicial proceedings are also permitted, and the making of a three-dimensional object from a two-dimensional art work need not be an infringement if it appears not to be a reproduction of that art work to the lay observer.

Typographical copyright

116   Part II of the Act is headed 'Copyright in sound recordings, cinematograph films, broadcasts etc'. After Sections 12 (sound recordings), 13 (cinematograph films), 14 (television and sound broadcasts), the 'etc.' is obviously meant to refer to typographical arrangement, which is the subject of Section 15, (Section 16, the only other one in this Part, deals with supplementary provisions of a general nature). The shoulder note is a little confusing, as it reads 'Copyright in published editions of works', a somewhat different concept from typographical arrangement, which is said in sub-section (5) to be the property protected by the Section, viz 'The act restricted . . . is the making . . . of a reproduction of the typographical arrangement of the edition'. Sub-section (4) gives exemption from the provisions to librarians making copies in accordance with Regulations issued by the Board of Trade. We have already considered these above.

Education

117   Section 41 is one of the 'Miscellaneous and supplementary provisions' constituting Part VI of the Act. It is headed 'Use of copyright materials for education'. It gives protection to teachers, but only in schools, using copyright material in the course of instruction — provided no duplicating equipment is used — and as part of the questions or answers for an examination — with no proviso about duplicating. Sub-section (2) makes clear that re-publication is not permitted by this Section. Sub-section (3) states that literary, dramatic and musical works may be performed in school provided the audience, if any, does not include outside persons. And outside

persons includes parents or guardians. Sub-section 7 offers definitions
of 'school' (as in the Education Act 1944 and parallel legislation for
Scotland and Northern Ireland) and 'duplicating process' (any device
for producing multiple copies).

Public records

118   Under Section 42 any work in copyright which is incorporated into
Public Records, may be copied by any officer appointed under the
Public Records acts without infringing copyright.

Substantiality

119   Under the heading 'Supplementary provisions as to interpretation'
(definitions etc. largely come into Section 48), Section 49 states in
sub-section (1) that for any act (e.g. of copying) to be recognised
under the Act it must involve a substantial part of the copyright work.
This section goes on in sub-section (2) to define publication in various
ways, but those of most interest to librarians are that in (2)(b), 'a
publication which is merely colourable, and not intended to serve the
reasonable requirements of the public, shall be disregarded', and in
(2)(c) 'a work . . . shall be taken to have been published if, but only
if, reproductions . . . have been issued to the public.'

General matters: term

120   The term of copyright in literary, dramatic and musical works is fixed
at 50 years after the end of the year in which the author died, in the
case of published works, and in perpetuity in the case of unpublished
works. Where an unpublished work is first published after an author's
death copyright subsists for 50 years after the end of the year of first
publication. In the latter case, performing the work, selling records
of it and broadcasting it are taken to have the same effect as publishing
it. Similar length of copyright protection is offered to authors of
artistic works, except photographs, where it lasts fifty years after the
end of the year of first publication. In the case of photographs this is
a change from the 1911 Act, which protected them for only 50 years
after being made. The 1956 Act is not retrospective and its extra
protection applies only to photographs made after 1st June 1957.

Ownership

121   The ownership of copyright is generally that of the author, but there
are exceptions. If a work is made for periodical publication in the
course of employment, under a contract of service or of employment,
and if the employer is a newspaper, magazine or periodical proprietor;
then copyright belongs to the proprietor, but only for that work's
publication in that form. A second exception is the commissioning for
payment of an artistic work, such as taking a photograph, painting or

drawing a portrait, or making an engraving. In these cases the copyright belongs to the commissioner. A third sub-section adds to these all similar work done under a contract of service or in course of employment. In these cases too, the copyright belongs to the employer. Later clauses deal with ownership or assignment of copyright, e.g. in Section 38, where it is stated to pass under will, and Section 39 in which Crown copyright is dealt with. Under this Section it is generally set out that works made under the direction of the Crown or a Government department or first published by the Government belong to the Crown. Duration of Crown copyright is for 50 years after the end of the year of first publication (in the case of literary works), but the Crown also holds perpetual copyright in its unpublished works. Librarians perplexed by whether a work is in or out of copyright are assisted by two other provisions in Section 11 of the Act. The first deals with anonymous and pseudonymous works. Under the second Schedule of the Act, the copyright in these lasts only for 50 years after the end of the year of publication, provided it is not possible to discover by 'reasonable enquiry' the author's identity at any time during that period. Works of joint authorship in which each author's contribution is indistinguishable from the other(s)' are protected until the end of fifty years after the end of the year of death of the author who died last. The third Schedule to the Act gives these last conditions in considerable detail.

Legal deposit

122   Finally in this chapter we must note the position of the law of legal deposit. No mention of it is made in the Copyright Act 1956, but the provisions in the Copyright Act 1911 were not repealed, and Section 15 of that Act remains the authority. It has seven sub-sections. The first requires every publisher to deliver at his own cost within one month of publication a copy of every book he publishes in the U.K. to the British Museum. This has been amended by Statutory Instrument to read British Library. Sub-section (2) requires the publisher also to deliver, if required within 12 months of publication, further copies to the Bodleian Library, the University Library, Cambridge, the National Library of Scotland (formerly the Advocates' Library) and the library of Trinity College Dublin. These copies must be delivered within one month of the request being made. The National Library of Wales is entitled to similar privileges to the other four, apart from some exceptions specified by order of the Board of Trade. The copy for the British Library is to be one of the best copies (if various editions are issued), those for other libraries are to be of the edition of which most copies are for sale. Fines not exceeding five pounds and the value of the book are levyable on summary conviction for failure to comply with the Section. Sub-section (7) defines 'book' as every part of a book, pamphlet, sheet of letterpress, sheet of music, map, plan, chart or table that are separately

published. Reprints and new editions are not required unless they contain additions or alterations. The 1924 Board of Trade Regulations for the National Library of Wales allow publishers of editions small in number and high in price (figures are cited) to withhold copies under legal deposit unless the book in question is either in Welsh or concerned principally with Welsh culture. The British Museum Library also obtained orders allowing it to decline to receive certain categories of printed matter, such as timetables, calendars, blank printed forms, etc., and this type of literature is not required for deposit.

2
Interpretations of the Copyright Act 1956

201 The interpretations offered in this chapter do not derive merely from a simple consideration of the Copyright Act and the Libraries Regulations as set out in the last chapter. They also rely heavily on both events and writings leading up to the Act and following its coming into force. Some interpretations, for example, hark back to the Gregory report, that was the immediate precursor of the Act, others look to commentaries such as those of *Photocopying and the law* and the Whitford report itself. Opinion on the law is always changing, even when, as here, there is no case law to provide new precedents. Nevertheless, it seems best to place interpretations here, close to the exposition of the law, rather than later after consideration of other commentaries, as probably being a more useful arrangement. Interpretations of the law relating to microforms, audiovisual materials and computers are included in the chapter devoted to those forms.

202 Here, in as rational an order as we can discover, I offer some opinions on what the law means to the librarian, in a series of questions and answers. This is a good place to repeat the warning that the opinions are not those of a qualified lawyer, except where one is quoted or cited, and are intended only as a guide to what seems reasonable in the way of actions or precautions. I am heavily indebted to a number of others who have written on the subject, and where possible these sources are referred to. The difficulty seems always to be that whereas the librarian as a rule knows little of the law, the lawyer frequently knows as little of libraries and can easily misunderstand the particular circumstances in which librarians find themselves. His professional advice therefore, is sometimes to be found not inaccurate but irrelevant. I hope that by taking the library situation first, and considering its legal implications, as far as I can elucidate them, I have managed to throw a little light into these corners without too many distorting shadows.

I The nature of copyright

203 **What does copyright protect?**
The expression of an idea, but not the idea itself. Virtually any

arrangement of words, images or sounds created in any way is first the copyright of its creator. The law of copyright protects everything from timetables to novels in the literary world, from the merest sketch to the largest canvas in graphic design, from notations to recordings in music, and the shapes of sculptures, models, artifacts and even buildings in the three-dimensional world (see 101).

204   Is there a copyright in book titles?
No. The title may itself be a piece of creative writing, but is regarded as a label only: it may be used for another work without infringing copyright. But, of course, if the creator of such a second work wished people to believe it was the first work, or an adaptation or somehow related to the first work, then the law against passing off one's work as though it was another's comes into play. But that is not itself copyright law.

205   Is there a copyright in facts?
No, but one might be called upon to prove that one was not copying an original source in presenting facts. For instance, if one publishes a bibliography of book titles derived from the British National Bibliography, it could be held to be unauthorised copying, even if the entries were neither completely identical nor in the same order, nor a complete reproduction of the whole source. Many years ago a publisher of a bibliographical list suspected unauthorised copying by another publisher. Proof was obtained by the inclusion in the first list of a 'spoof' entry, which duly turned up in the second list. In short, if the expression or arrangement of your facts is owed substantially to an original source, you could be infringing copyright. It is an extension of the old saying 'to copy one author is plagiarism; to copy two is research'.

206   What acts infringe copyright?
Briefly the copying in a tangible form of the original, or a substantial part of it. There are many exceptions to this rule, such as 'fair dealing', and additions which will be gone into later, such as performance, broadcast, etc., of a work which can be an infringement though no tangible form exists of the 'copying', and the making of hand-written copies privately, which is not an infringement.

207   Does the whole of a work have to be copied before there is an infringement of copyright?
No, copying a substantial part or more of a work constitutes an infringement unless there is a defence on other grounds.

208   How much can I copy before it is a substantial part?
One of the problems facing users of copyright material is vagueness in the terms used in the law. Although the 1956 Act has a section of

definitions (Section 48), 'substantial part', 'reasonable part' and 'fair dealing' are not included. Therefore they must be given interpretation as words in common use. Here the legal commentaries are of some help. There were some pre-1911 court decisions that can be tacitly taken to be incorporated into the 1911 and 1956 Acts that held quantity not the only factor in deciding what was a substantial part. If the part copied contained the essence of the whole, or a summary of it, or if a vital table or calculation was included, or in the case of music, if a few bars that carried the principal melody were copied, then it could be held that a substantial part was taken, and an infringement had been made.

209 Can one make a paraphrase of a work without infringing copyright?
This circumstance is not likely to arise frequently in the work of a librarian, except when he may want to abridge, adapt, revise, etc., some work for private use. In these instances he is acting not as a librarian but as an administrator or a private scholar. The embargo on unauthorised adaptation is essentially against the production of competing works. The question of abstracts is considered later (292). The main point to be observed is that infringement of copyright, although it cannot include copying of ideas, is not limited to verbatim copying of the original, but can include imitations or works of a parallel nature based on and serving the same ends as the original. Précis and brief digests of works are not normally considered infringement, if they incorporate the original work of summarising. To reproduce the headings of a sectionalised work as a summary, on the other hand, may not be allowable. Here the test would be one of originality in the secondary work.

210 How can one decide whether a work is published or unpublished?
This can be a difficult decision in special cases, but the normal meaning of publication is taken to be the production of sufficient copies made available to satisfy the reasonable requirements of the public. The production of a book in a limited edition is generally assumed to be publication, but there may be doubts over restricted editions. For example, if copies are available only to members of a society, but that society's membership is open to anyone who wishes to join, one would suppose its publications to have been published. But private circulation to hand-picked individuals would probably be regarded as not constituting publication. For microform publication see 707.

211 Does a work forfeit its copyright if the publisher ignores legal deposit?
No, copyright subsists in a published work on publication, and in an unpublished work in perpetuity. The legal deposit requirements (122) have no bearing on copyright, though they are included in the Copyright Act 1911. The fact that the deposit libraries are sometimes

known as the copyright libraries similarly confers no benefit on them in respect of copyright, nor does it impose any obligations connected with copyright.

II Whose is the copyright?

212 If I publish a book while employed as a librarian, whose is the copyright?

This will depend on one's conditions of employment. Normally, any work produced in the course of one's duties under a contract of service or apprenticeship is the copyright of the employer. Librarians should be wary of cases where their published work is based on materials kept at their place of work, even though not all, or any, of the work was done in their employers' time. Such cases are arguable, and a clear understanding beforehand is preferable to dispute afterwards. In cases of other employment contracts, the copyright of works or products or by-products of the work is negotiable.

213 How can I distinguish a publication that is in copyright from one that is out of copyright?

If the author is alive, it is in copyright; if he is dead it will be in copyright until the end of fifty years after the year in which he died. For example the works of Joseph Conrad, who died on 3rd August 1924, came out of copyright on 1st January 1975, those of Thomas Hardy, who died on 11th January 1928, came out of copyright on 1st January 1979. There are several qualifications to this rule, however, as follows.

214 What is the copyright of a posthumous work?

It extends fifty years from the end of the year of publication. Thus Robert Tressell died in 1911, and the first publication of *The Ragged Trousered Philanthropists* was in 1914. Copyright in that publication ceased on 1st January 1965, but the 1914 edition was incomplete, and the full text was not published until 1955. At that time the new publishers had to seek permission to reprint those parts that had appeared in 1914, but had their own copyright in the previously unpublished material. Since the first abridged edition is now out of copyright the only copyright remaining is in the new material. There is no typographical arrangement copyright in this edition as it was published before 1st June 1957 when that new provision of the 1956 Act took effect.

215 Who owns the copyright in a collection of unpublished letters deposited in a library?

Normally the author of each letter or his heirs. The recipient has no copyright in them unless it has been specifically assigned. It is not automatically acquired by the library with their deposit. Thus a collection of letters from 100 different writers to the same person is copyright, until published, by the 100 writers. The varying dates of death of the writers makes no difference: copyright under the 1956 Act is perpetual until first publication, after which it lasts a further fifty years after the year of publication.

216   But these letters have been in the library for generations: are there no exceptions to this rule?
Yes, if the author has been dead for at least fifty years *and* if the letters (this also applies to any unpublished documents) were written at least 100 years ago, then some use may be made of them. They can be photocopied or otherwise reproduced for research or private study. All this applies only to libraries that are open to public inspection, and of course only where the depositor of the manuscripts has not stipulated that such use should be prohibited.

217   If the researcher or student then wishes to publish the letters or other manuscripts, is it permitted?
Yes, provided the publisher announces his intention to do so at least twice, not less than three months on the first occasion and two months on the second before publication. The announcements must be in either a daily or a Sunday newspaper with national circulation (see 104).

218   Who does the copyright belong to then?
The original owner of the copyright still has his rights, but the first publisher also has a copyright in the part or parts of the work he has published. For example, in the case of a library publishing a selection of poems from a manuscript in its care, if the correct steps, as outlined above, have been taken, the library has not committed an infringement in the event of a rightful copyright owner appearing after publication. But the copyright owner can also publish the same selection or a different one. The library could in that case reprint or modify its original text, but it cannot include any new matter from the manuscript.

219   How is the law interpreted in the case of joint authorship?
Where two or more authors' contributions to a jointly authored work are indistinguishable, copyright lasts until fifty years after the year of death of the owner who died last. Where contributions are separately attributable, each author has his own copyright. Thus the music in Gilbert and Sullivan's operas came out of copyright in 1951 as Sullivan died in 1900, but the words were released into the public domain only in 1962, as Gilbert died in 1911.

220   Is there a copyright in anonymous works?
Yes, this lasts for fifty years after the end of the year of publication,

provided that it is not possible to discover the identity of the author at any time before the end of that fifty years. The same rule applies to pseudonymous works, but not to works by joint authors unless all the authors are either anonymous or pseudonymous.

221 Are government publications copyrighted?
In this country, they are, though not in the United States. In fact the Crown claims at present the copyright in all works published or unpublished, by the Government or its Departments, whether written by individual authors or not (see 121).

222 What is the position of foreign publications?
The United Kingdom, as a signatory of the Berne and Universal Copyright Conventions, offers the same protection to foreign publications as it does to British ones, provided that the country where the work was published is also a signatory of one of the Conventions. There are now no significant producers of published works excluded from both the Berne and U.C.C. so one can take the position that for all practical purposes the 1956 Act applies universally: this merely does a little more than justice to the few countries outside the Conventions. However, as mentioned above, the United States claims no copyright for its own government publications and it would be unreasonable to expect prospective users to seek permission merely because British law requires it. The question of what constitutes a U.S. government publication is considered later in the chapter on United States copyright law (804).

223 How does one discover whether an author is in copyright?
For literary writers there are biographical dictionaries and literary histories that usually give years of birth and death. In borderline cases it is advisable to check in more than one source, since reference books occasionally err. Lesser known or specialist writers can sometimes be looked up in works on their subject. In all cases of failure, the prospective user should write to the publisher at the address given in the book to be copied, preferably checking it in a current directory of publishers. If the publisher is no longer in business or cannot be traced, users should write to the Publishers Association or the Society of Authors for information on the present copyright owners. These bodies will perhaps be unable to give the answer, but since they do have a considerable amount of information (indeed the Society of Authors acts as literary executor for a number of authors' heirs), this step should not be omitted.

224 Can a library copy a modern edition of a classic work?
If an author's copyright has expired there may still be a copyright in typographical arrangement, whereby the publisher may restrain unfettered photographic or facsimile copying of the printed page. This

right lasts for 25 years after the year of first publication of the particular typesetting, but it does not apply to any works printed before 1st June 1957, the first day of operation of the Copyright Act 1956. If a publisher should himself reproduce in a facsimile version a work previously published prior to 1st June 1957, or more than 25 years ago, he has no copyright in the typography except of course in any new matter such as preliminaries, introductions or indexes. The wording of the Act in one place speaks of 'published editions' but this is misleading. If a scholar edits a classic work so that the text is different from those previously published he or anyone to whom he has assigned the right will have a separate right (life plus 50 years) in his text and the publisher will also have the 25 year right in the typography of the printed page. In the case of an annotated but otherwise unchanged text, the out-of-copyright text may be copied freely, but the notes will bear the editor's copyright as an author, and the publisher may well have typographic arrangement copyright.

225 Is the author always the person to approach for copyright permission?
No, in fact it is usually better to approach the publisher, unless the whereabouts of the author are more readily discoverable. Copyright may be assigned by the author at any time, and in certain classes of publication full rights are more usually held by the publisher. These include contributions, whether signed or not, to encyclopaedias and similar commissioned pieces of writing.

226 Who holds copyright in periodicals?
The normal state of affairs is for the publisher to hold copyright in matter produced 'in house' and for authors of articles to hold their own copyright. But the 'normal' state is unfortunately not as usual as it might be. Although there has in recent years been a tendency towards authors explicitly retaining their own rights, or some of them, frequently there is no contract between publisher and author, or the publisher demands full rights. Where no contract exists it is generally held that the publisher has full rights for serial publication. However, when a periodical article is required for inclusion in, say, an anthology, it is usual to request permission from the original serial publisher. If he is aware of not holding rights himself, he will consult the author. It is thus best to approach the publisher for all permissions to copy. Copyright in serials will last as for other works: anonymous material for fifty years after the year of publication, and signed or attributable pieces for fifty years after the year of the author's death. Thus a single issue can carry many different lengths of copyright.

227 What are the copyrights in audio-visual materials?
These are so complex that they are given a separate chapter: one physical entity can carry several different copyrights. See chapter 7 (716-66).

III   Fair dealing

228   What does fair dealing mean in the context of the Copyright law?
There is no certainty in the matter of fair dealing, and it will be best
to try to elucidate what it means for librarians stage by stage. First,
the simple meaning of the words. There is no definition in the 1956
Act, nor was there one in the 1911 Act which also used the phrase.
Therefore it means what the words signify in common speech,
modified by any cases that have come to court. In general it appears
that there is no need to seek the protection of 'fair dealing' if a
substantial part is not copied, since there would be no infringement —
though we must remember the complexities of what is a substantial
part. But if a substantial part is copied, then a defence of fair dealing
may be valid. In such circumstances this seems to depend on whether
the copying competes with the original. However even if an act of
copying can claim to be non-competitive, it is not clear that no
infringement takes place. The 1956 Act limits exceptions under fair
dealing to three specific purposes: for research or private study, for
criticism or review, and for reporting current events. There are other
general exceptions, such as reproducing for judicial purposes, or
including short passages in schools' collections, but these are not
described as fair dealing.

229   What does fair dealing mean to librarians?
The second two conditions under which fair dealing is not an infringement are easily disposed of, and will rarely concern librarians.
Criticisms and reviews are generally publications, though presumably
the writer may ask librarians to provide photocopies for this purpose,
and the exception is for writers' protection against the infringement
of publication. The Society of Authors and Publishers Association
in 1958 issued a 'Fair dealing statement' setting out limits within
which they considered 'objection could not normally be taken'. Beyond
these limits of quotation, a reviewer or critic would be expected to
apply for permission. In the case of fair dealing for reporting current
events, there could be a closer relevance for those librarians, for
example who issue to their users a current awareness service that
includes news extracts.

230   The main question, however, is whether libraries can shelter under
the first sub-section of Section 6 which reads, in its entirety:

> 'No fair dealing with a literary, dramatic or musical work for
> purposes of research or private study shall constitute an infringe-
> ment of the copyright in the work'.

The wording is very straightforward, merely begging the question of
definitions. 'Research', 'private study' and 'fair dealing' are all
undefined, either here or in Section 48 which deals with special

meanings of words and phrases used in the Act. Were it not for the existence of Section 7 (Special exceptions as respects libraries and archives), there could be no question but that Section 6 applied generally, since it carries no restrictions as to who may perform the fair dealing. Were there no Section 7, Section 6 could be read by librarians to imply that any users of any library could have copies made for him of substantial extracts, or even of complete works, provided the purpose of the copying were research or private study, and provided the copying did not substitute for a purchase of the original or tend towards competing unfairly with the original. There are those who claim that this is the intention of the Act, or at least that the Act permits this practice. G. Woledge, for example (ref. 20, p.29) says 'Since the provisions of Section 6 (fair dealing) allow all that is needed, it is hard to see why any librarian should make use of the more cumbrous procedure of Section 7 unless he feels that his judgement of what is fair cannot be trusted'. He goes on to reinforce this view when discussing copying from books: 'procedure under Section 7 is of very limited help, and most likely copying will have to be justified under Section 6'.

231   This approach seems over-legalistic, not to say cynical. It assumes that Section 7 can be ignored when convenient because of a loophole in Section 6. Certainly when the wording of Section 6 is examined there is a loophole (not the only one in the Act) as we have seen, and one wonders if a case that used this loophole as a defence would be lost. However, the wording of Section 7 is so precise, and the conditions under which library copying is permitted so much more constricted, that I find it impossible to believe that the drafters of the Act intended that libraries should wriggle out of its constraints to shelter under the general fair dealing provision. D. C. Pearce, in supporting this line of argument states: 'The approach adopted by the courts when interpreting statutes is that if special provisions dealing with a clearly recognizable class of individuals are included in an Act without any indication that general provisions in the Act are also to apply to those persons, then the general provisions are to be regarded as excluded.' (ref. 150) Although Pearce was speaking of the Australian situation, I believe his remarks are valid for the British.

232   Unfortunately for those who take the view that library copying should be rather restricted to what is permitted in Section 7, a precedent has been quoted that carries little conviction; indeed Mr. Woledge shows in an Appendix to the article quoted how irrelevant it is. In fact the first version of *Photocopying and the law* confidently asserts 'Legal precedent, however, has established that such fair dealing must be exercised by the individual for himself, and not by any one person on behalf of another'. This is modified in the 1970 text (after

Woledge's article) to 'There is, however, some authority for holding that such fair dealing etc. . . . '

233   If one goes back to the Gregory Report, the intentions of the Committee are quite clear: the fair dealing provision is not for libraries:

> 'What comes within the 'fair dealing' exemption if done by the student himself (and in this respect no alteration is proposed) [i.e. to the 1911 Act] would not necessarily be covered if done by the librarian'.

> 'We recommend that, subject to the conditions set out below, any action which would come within the description of 'fair dealing' if done by the student himself, should be so regarded if done by a librarian acting on his behalf'.

234   But the 'conditions set out below' are in essence and substance the provisions later incorporated into Section 7 of the 1956 Act. The Gregory Committee sees a clear distinction between copying periodical articles and extracts from books, and positively recommends that copyright permission should always be sought by librarians when making 'substantial part' copies from books.

235   If we may offer an additional gloss on the matter, it could probably be held that in these days of short run printing, library copying facilities are a more significant element in the total distribution pattern of documents than they were before, say, 1960, and the advent of xerography. As Peter G. New puts it 'the multiplication of texts is nowadays not confined to the publisher/printer combination: it is also taking place lower down the information chain nearer the point of use, e.g. by libraries, information centres, and the user himself' (ref. 32) To put it shortly, the existence of a library with its wide-ranging stock, and on-the-spot quick copying facilities, is itself a negation of any 'fair dealing' situation, because the library is competing, or offering to compete, with the original publisher. If not exactly competition, this facility may alternatively be termed parasitic supplementation of the original publication. By either definition exploitation without reward is a feature of the action.

236   I make no apology for the length of this excursus on libraries and fair dealing: it is the key to the interpretations of the Act and Regulations which now follow. My view may not be good news for librarians in general, but it may be found in subsequent interpretations that the limits to dissemination that it suggests are not quite as inhibiting to research and information work as they appear at first.

IV The Libraries Regulations

237 Can any library operate under the Copyright (Libraries) Regulations?
No, the categories allowed are explicit, though there may be some
dispute over interpreting the meaning of the last group. The libraries
are specified in the first schedule of the Regulations in five groups:

    (a) legal deposit libraries
    (b) educational libraries
    (c) public, rate supported, libraries
    (d) parliamentary and government department libraries
    (e) libraries for the study of various subjects (a list (106) embrac-
         ing virtually all subject fields; business is not listed, but could
         perhaps be included as social science, which is).

Section 1 of the Regulations adds the all-important proviso that
libraries conducted for profit are not included.

238 What types of library are excluded?
Private schools and colleges, apart from those precluded from making
a profit by virtue of being registered charities, or philanthropic
organisations; commercial lending libraries; libraries of public
corporations (e.g. the gas, steel and water industries) which are
expected to make a profit; libraries of private firms, commercial and
industrial. It has occasionally been argued that in all these instances,
except that of the commercial lending library, the library is not
conducted for profit though the firm is, but this argument is not
generally accepted (240).

239 How may excluded libraries make the most of their disadvantages?
(1) by remembering that much copying, though not of whole
periodical articles, may be permissible as not constituting a substantial
part.
(2) by arranging that a self-service copying machine on which
researchers and private students may make their own copies under the
fair dealing exceptions, is available elsewhere in the organisation.
(3) by coming to private licensing arrangements with publishers, e.g.
of the most frequently requested journals.
(4) by making it formally open to the public, the librarian puts his
library in the category of those which may supply copies under the
Libraries Regulations to other libraries though they may not receive
copies. The advantage of this provision is not always apparent.
(5) by taking advantage of the general licence of the British Copyright
Council in *Photocopying and the law* (305-8). A librarian can suggest
to publishers that they permit him these privileges, which though
advocated by, are not strictly authorisable by the BCC. However,
conforming to the limits set out by *Photocopying and the law* would

be a cogent defence were a case to be brought, even if the library had not made direct approaches to publishers.

(6) by taking advantage of the limited permissions given by the Royal Society's fair dealing declaration, 3rd ed. 1957. The Royal Society regards this document as largely inoperative but it was issued, unlike its predecessors, without a time limit, and is still presumably valid for the publishers and periodicals listed, except where later publishers' statements explicitly contradict it.

240 **What is the purpose of excluding for-profit libraries from the operation of the Regulations?**
The Gregory Committee felt that copying of less than a substantial part was sufficient licence for a library's unfettered copying. Researchers and private students could obtain better exemptions provided they were not assisted by libraries. If further privileges were to be sought by library users, it was necessary to ensure that publishers' and authors' interests did not suffer. By limiting the extra copying facilities to libraries mostly in the public sector and with no commercial interest to serve, the Gregory Committee must have thought an added safeguard was being introduced.

241 A rather simplistic view of industry and commerce must have prevailed, in which all actions of profit-making companies were seen to be potentially essentially profitable actions, and quite different from those of non-profit institutions. The whole tradition of public library service to industry, in which industry and commerce are seen as national assets to be nourished by public services is tacitly set at nought.

242 In practical terms, the user of a commercial or industrial library can go to a public library, or any academic library to which he has access, and obtain as a researcher or private student that which the regulations forbid his own company library to supply. Public and private interests in research are so intermixed that it is generally agreed that this was one area where the Gregory Committee was short-sighted. The legislators who followed them blindly accepted their recommendation, though we are told by Mr. Woledge that an amending recommendation in Parliament was refused, that would specifically have included non-profit libraries of profit-making companies in the list of prescribed libraries. This suggests that Parliament intended such libraries not to have the privileges of the Regulations, though Mr. Woledge says 'it might perhaps be argued that they are not in fact included' among the unprivileged libraries. What we have to remember is that the Regulations were made later by the Board of Trade and not at the specific dictate of Parliament. Whether by oversight or intention it is sufficiently clear that the exclusion is to stand.

243 **How much of a periodical is a prescribed library allowed to copy?**

The rules specify that no more than one article in any one publication may be copied. An 'article' is defined in the Act as an item of any kind. This allows one to copy an editorial, a regular feature, an illustrative feature, or even the index. The phrase 'one publication' is generally taken to mean one part or issue of a periodical. Thus separate copies from different issues of the same volume could be taken for the same user. However, one would not extend this freedom to 'double' or multiple issues unless they were internally divided, so as to show where one issue began and another ceased. In the case of one article comprising the whole of a periodical issue, there is no restriction against copying the whole article, though the Gregory Committee specifically recommend that 'the copy supplied does not constitute substantially the whole issue, but is restricted to not more than one article'. The proviso must have been thought to be too imprecise by the Regulations drafters and the first part of it has been dropped. One article spread over two or more issues may of course be copied at the one time since there is no restriction against copying from more than one issue. Similarly one article comprising the whole or a major part of a 'double' issue may also be copied in full.

244   **What is to be done for users requiring two or more articles from one part?**
The answer to this question must necessarily appear shifty. The correct procedure, and one that should be mentioned first, is that the user or library should purchase a second copy of the periodical part, to lend or supply, not to copy from. If it is unobtainable, permission to copy should be sought from the publisher. It is unclear whether a library can copy two articles from one part if it has two copies of the part — probably not. However, there are other ways in which a library may legally respond. The user may be advised to return on another occasion for the second request. He may be lent the periodical for a short period, during which as a private student or researcher he may make his own copies, by whatever means are available to him.

245   What is not permitted is for the user to employ an agent to obtain the extra copy for him, since the person making the request must be the person for whom the copies are intended. Nor is it permitted for the library to make all the required copies at one time and supply them one at a time. It is not made clear how much time should elapse between the making of one legal copy from a periodical part and the copying of a second article from the same part for the same person: the Act and the Regulations are silent on this point, so that it could be argued that a person is *never* entitled to a second article. However, a usual interpretation is that a second article could be supplied if say a week has passed, and the request is clearly a separate occasion.

246   The purpose of the restriction is clearly to defend copyright, and

prevent copying from substituting for purchase of the original. It is frequently the case that a periodical will issue a special number in which several articles are on the same or a related subject. Readers generally interested in the subject may want copies of two or more articles whereas the more particular enquirer or researcher is more likely to need only one. The law favours the latter at the expense of the former, perhaps because general interest is less likely to further the advancement of learning than particular research.

247 What types of publication can be called periodicals for the purposes of copying articles from them?
The generally accepted definition is that any publication issued at intervals, with no set completion in prospect can be termed a periodical. Frequency or regularity does not come into the question at all. A periodical can be anything from daily to once every five years or more provided it can be seen to be a continuing entity. Obviously a series of books issued, say, at one a month is not a periodical, though here a case might conceivably be argued if other characteristics of a periodical were apparent, such as an overall title, a subscription price, a numbering sequence, consistency of type presentation. The literary periodicals *Life and letters* and *Horizon* for instance published one or two complete works, later issued as books, as whole issues. It would be permitted to copy these, but of course, only from the periodical versions.

248 Annual or (other frequency) conferences consisting of papers and proceedings can be treated as periodicals provided they form part of a continuing publication. So too can annual or other reviews of progress or the 'Advances in . . . ' type of publication. Even though they are sold separately and not on subscription it can be well argued that these are periodicals. Not all the features of a periodical need to be present, just sufficient of them to give the overall character. But the categorising of regular conference proceedings as periodicals does not extend to 'one off' events. Conference and seminar proceedings may be treated as periodicals only if their publication is part of a series. The fact that a conference was published separately only once, and the other times in a periodical, would not however, I think, invalidate the periodical character, though a conference proceedings that was published separately once and the other times not at all or dispersed through other journals probably would not count as a periodical. Symposia of articles on a broad or narrow topic should not be treated as periodicals unless some other periodical characteristic is present. Similarly part works, designed to be completed in a set number of issues, even if that number is unknown at the beginning, are not strictly speaking periodicals, even, again, though they consist of short separate articles, such as encyclopaedia part works. It might however, be claimed that they could be copied as periodicals during the period of issue though not thereafter, but the matter is obscure and guidance should be sought from the publisher.

249   A final point about bound volumes: whether a periodical is bound in a set or still in separate parts makes no difference to the operation of the Regulations. Two or more articles can be copied if in different parts even though the parts are bound up.

250   **Under the Regulations how much of a non-periodical item may be copied by a library for a user?**
Anything less than a substantial part (208) may be copied without recourse to the Regulations at all, since only copying a substantial part can constitute an infringement. When a prescribed library is supplying a researcher or private student it may copy 'a reasonable part' of a work if copyright ownership cannot be traced. Finding no explanation of the term 'reasonable part' except that it can be more than a 'substantial part', in the Act or Regulations, we turn to the Gregory Report and are little better served. Their view was that an extract should 'not represent an unreasonably large part of the whole work and [should be] kept strictly to the minimum needs of the reader of a particular study'.

251   Were a case to be brought against a library for copying more than a reasonable part, there would be no defence available from definition in the Act or Regulations, or in the Gregory Report, nor has there been a case to provide a precedent. The only defence we can suggest would be if the part copied fell within the guidelines suggested in *Photocopying and the law* (405-8). In that case, however, it could also perhaps be claimed that the part copied was not even substantial. The difficulty is that there are three levels of copying, two of them overlapping, envisaged in the Act, (a) less than a substantial part, (b) a substantial part but admissible under fair dealing for private study or research and (c) a reasonable part. *Photocopying and the law* offers only one quantity (405) which applies both to 'fair dealing' and 'a reasonable part'. The British Copyright Council has however not equated the two conditions above this minimum level. What, above this level, might be permitted to a private student copying for himself is not necessarily free from prosecution if done by a library as a reasonable part, since there could be cases where fair dealing could permit copying a complete work, and this is hardly likely to be interpreted as a reasonable part.

252   A library then finds itself in the position of having to apply for copying permission for all copying in excess of limits set out in *Photocopying and the law*. If the copyright owner cannot be traced, and if the library goes ahead and copies what it considers a reasonable part, it will not have any automatic protection from later prosecution,

and its only defence will be its judgement of what is a reasonable part. This was hardly the position intended by the Gregory Committee or the drafters of the Act, which notes that the Regulations should 'include such provisions as the Board of Trade may consider appropriate for securing that no copy to which the Regulations apply extends to more than a reasonable proportion of the work in question'. The Regulations, however, merely repeat the phrase 'a reasonable proportion'. Small wonder that many libraries refuse to copy beyond the limits of *Photocopying and the law.*

253 There seems to be no prohibition in the Act or Regulations against copying a complete work in stages for an individual applying to a library on separate occasions — ten would be needed at least under *Photocopying and the law*'s limits. But this would be quite clearly against the spirit and intention of the Act and Regulations, and librarians noticing this going on would be well advised to put a stop to it. However, the resourceful would-be copier could still achieve his aim by going to different libraries.

254 **How much may a library copy for another library?**
Almost anything, but certain conditions are attached. Only libraries prescribed (106, 237) or libraries freely open to the public may make copies, and copies may not be supplied to libraries established or conducted for profit. It appears that a library that makes its materials freely available to the public, as many special libraries do, is still not permitted to receive copies, if it belongs to a profit-making organisation. Again, as before (238, 241) arguments could be adduced on the other side. The purpose of this limited extension of the franchise for making copies is that many company libraries contain unique or rare materials that should be made available to the scholarly world at large. Potential profiteering by such libraries is excluded by the proviso that the libraries must be open freely to the public, but there is no restraint on the charges they may make for any copies themselves that the library may make. Further conditions are that copyright permission must be obtained, except for periodical article copying, or where not obtained reasonable enqiury must be made to discover the copyright owner, only one copy may be made, unless a previously supplied copy can be established as lost, destroyed or damaged, and charges must be made for the copies, at not less than cost plus a contribution to library overheads.

255 One strange effect of the rather ramshackle way in which the Regulations are drafted is that there seems to be no restriction on libraries supplying more than one article from a periodical part to another library. However, the oddity remains that if a library has in stock a periodical part it may copy for its own user only one article, whereas if it does not have that part in stock it may request more than

one article in it from another library. The receiving library may not, however, supply more than one article to its user at one time. Such awkwardnesses abound in the Regulations probably because of the drafters' failure to realise the needs and practices of libraries and their users.

256 In the case of non-periodical items, there is none of the hazard of the lack of definition of 'reasonable part' because libraries may copy for each other as much as the whole of a work, provided they have been unable to trace the copyright owner.

257 **What are the rules about charging for photocopies?**
In their concern for the interests of copyright owners, the Gregory Committee suggests libraries should charge for making copies: 'The charge which will necessarily be made by a library authorised to copy under our recommendation should safeguard the sales of the publisher, since a person who would normally buy the periodical would not be tempted to secure it by copying rather than by purchase in the ordinary course'. The recommendation suggested by the Committee and taken up in the Act and the Regulations is that in the case of both supplying to individuals and supplying to libraries, the supplying library must make a charge of not less than the cost of making the copies together with a contribution to the overheads of the library.

258 Mr. Woledge has pointed out (ref. 19, p.53) that the use of the plural number in the wording of the Regulation means that libraries can establish a fixed charge which taking one copy with another meets the condition of not making a loss. Most libraries do in fact charge a fixed fee per page copied or per sheet of photocopy, any difference lying in whether the copied sheet is large enough to take two printed pages. There is, however, nothing to prevent libraries making different charges for different copying jobs, e.g. for when the paper used is larger or smaller, or when a cheaper or more expensive process is used (e.g. for originals with half-tones or without). In fact the British Library Reference Division offers two types of copy, photographic or xerographic, and its charges vary accordingly.

259 It is also in order to vary the charge according to whether the work copied is in copyright or not, since libraries are not obliged to charge for making non-copyright copies. It can also be argued that copies of less than a substantial part of copyright originals need not be charged for by libraries, since the Regulations need not be invoked. But it is not usual to find this practice.

260 What constitutes the cost of making the copy is a matter of debate. certainly the paper, copying materials and a proportion of any rental or hire purchase of the machine should be included. It would also seem reasonable to add a proportion of the machine operator's salary, but some libraries may reckon that as part of the general overheads, to be taken into account when assessing the general expenses of the library towards which photocopying of copyright items must make a contribution.

261 Should VAT be charged on photocopies?

Yes. Photocopying is subject to VAT at standard rate, but the final cost of the copy as calculated should be without VAT. At the time of writing a further 15% should be added to arrive at the final charge to the recipient. However, because of the small sums involved, it is quite likely that a library's tariff will be rounded up to a convenient sum per page or sheet with VAT included. It should be noted that if a library charges for other photocopies, e.g. on non-copyrightable items, VAT must still be charged, even though the charge is not fixed under the Copyright Regulations.

262 Must the recipient of a copy sign a form and if so what is required on the form?

For all copies made by libraries for individuals under the Regulations a formal declaration must be signed. When a library copies for another library, no declaration is needed. But the copying library must satisfy itself that the receiving library has had no other copy of the work before, unless it has been lost, destroyed or damaged, and a declaration to this effect might reasonably be requested. No form is required for non-copyright copies, though some libraries ask for forms of the same nature to be completed for their own records. The British Copyright Council document *Photocopying and the law* advises all libraries taking advantage of their general licence to obtain declarations from photocopy recipients, even those libraries specifically excluded from the Regulations' scope. A user sometimes objects to the wording of the form in cases where the material is out of copyright and no obligations on the user of the copy need be imposed — such as using it only for private study or research. In these cases the library should modify the form appropriately, though it may require a signature from the recipient as an internal record. Only in libraries that are obliged by other laws or regulations to provide copies of documents out of copyright to the public may a user legitimately refuse altogether to sign a declaration. Such cases are unlikely to be met with, as the Public Libraries and Museums Act 1964 does not compel libraries to offer a photocopying service. Though it is clearly a service that is generally available, it is not specifically prescribed in the Act, and therefore is not exempt from what reasonable regulations the library may impose. The doubtful cases are more likely to arise in record offices and official archives.

263   The content of the required declaration is set out in Schedule Three of the Regulations. The essential elements are:

(1) The name and address of the user
(2) Making the request for the copy
(3) Identifying the item to be copied
(4) Stating the purpose as for research or private study
(5) Stating that no previous copy has been received from any library
(6) Stating that if the copy is supplied the user will not use it except for research or private study
(7) Signature of user, not stamped or typewritten, and not the signature of an agent of the user
(8) Date of request

264   **How far is the copyright in typographic arrangement protected against photocopying?**

Under the Regulations for libraries it is expressly stated that nothing otherwise permitted by the Regulations can be an infringement of the typographic arrangement copyright. In the case of 'fair dealing' under Section 6, by individual researcher or private student, there is no apparent protection. This suggests that users of self-service copiers who take copies of a part permitted under 'fair dealing' are nevertheless infringing the copyright in typographic arrangement. Although there is some support for this view in that under the 1911 Act 'fair dealing' copying was more likely to be performed by hand or typewriting, yet the Gregory Committee do not appear to have made this interpretation, as in para 43 they refer with satisfaction to the improved facilities for students that contact and microphotography have brought about. They seem to regard the distinction between hand and photographic copying as one of degree rather than kind, observing that while it is very well for students individually to have this facility the scale of copying that is opened up for libraries poses a different problem. For this reason it seems best to take the line that Mr Woledge takes, that this 'illogical restriction is perhaps an unintended consequence of the drafting of the Act'.

265   This line of thinking is reinforced by the absurdities that are also pointed out by Mr. Woledge (ref. 20, p47-8), that since the Regulations for libraries apply only to copyright works, this exemption does not apply in the case of a work that is itself out of copyright where there is a copyright in the typographical arrangement. Mr. Woledge notes other minor anomalies, but this one is surely decisive in justifying a general interpretation that libraries should be permitted to make copies of all works protected by typographical arrangement copyright only, as if the literary, etc., work was also in copyright, and that 'fair dealing' exceptions for students and others should also have an exemption from typographic arrangement copyright.

266 This means in practice that if a library is asked to take a copy of a complete or 'unreasonably large' part of a non-copyright work, it must take that copy from an edition that is itself not protected by the copyright of typographic arrangement (116) or if this is not possible, obtain permission to do so.

V Other queries on copying of textual matter

267 This section includes discussion of problems not immediately posed by wording of the Act and Regulations, which have nevertheless to be interpreted by what light can be had from them, together with any comments made by other authorities.

268 **What legal standing has the pamphlet 'Photocopying and the law'?**
None. However, were a court case to be brought on the grounds that more than a substantial part had been copied, it appears likely that a defence that the amount copied had been within these guidelines would probably carry some weight. But it should be remembered that neither the Publishers Association nor the Society of Authors has 100% membership of publishers or authors, and several groups of copyright owners, for instance music publishers and composers, are only lightly represented. Where a publication carries a warning notice that no part may be copied, although such a warning claims more protection than the law allows, it would be unwise to rely on *Photocopying and the law* as a protection. In its favour is the fact that the recommendations were published in 1965 and have not yet been openly repudiated by any publisher. It seems likely that the pamphlet would carry more weight on such a point as the interpretation of the legal language of 'substantial part' than if it were appealed to as justification for a for-profit library making copies for its users.

269 **What is a library's responsibility for self-service coin-operated machines?**
The placing of a photocopier that can be used by the public or users of a library, either inside the library premises or near to them, must permit the assumption that it can be intended for copying from works contained in the library, even if it is not exclusively for that purpose. A librarian or other person in charge of such a machine therefore carries some responsibility for seeing that copyright in works in the library is not infringed by users of the machine. If the machine is self-service, a notice clearly displayed is the least that can be done to guard against infringements. Some would say that periodical observations or sample surveys among the users should also be made, and if infringements are occurring, stricter supervision of its use should be introduced. *Photocopying and the law* states that librarians 'remain responsible for machines operated on their premises' and if a

case were to be brought it could be either jointly against the user and the librarian or the librarian alone if the user could not be discovered.

270   A notice should clearly state that the unfair copying of copyright works may render the copier liable to prosecution. Since the public or library user rarely knows what is permitted, the notice should further give guidance, such as that from the pamphlet *Photocopying and the law* on the recommended proportions of a work that can be copied or an instruction to seek advice from the library staff (provided they are in a position to give it). It would be advisable also to remind users of the separate copyright in anthology items such as poems, or separate artistic works. Self-service machines should, it is generally agreed, be considered as operating under the 'fair dealing' provisions of Section 6 rather than the library regulations, so complete items such as periodical articles should not be made unless they can be justified as 'fair dealing' for purposes of research or private study. Above all, the self-service copier should carry a warning against multiple copying, which cannot be 'fair dealing'. It could also be an infringement of typographic arrangement copyright even if the work was out of copyright, since multiple copying is not permitted under the Libraries Regulations. Multiple would in this instance include a second copy made after some interval of time from the first.

271   There is no statutory form of notice, but the British Copyright Council has issued a sheet suitable for display in a vertical format $14\frac{1}{2}$ x $8\frac{1}{2}$ inches, which carries the essential information, the text of which is reproduced as an appendix to this book.

272   **Can a library make copies of items for its own stock?**
The position in this is curious. A library has a wide scope (105-11) in making copies for other libraries, under Section 5 of the Libraries Regulations (and Section 7 of the Act), but there is no mention of making copies for its own stock in either Act or Regulations.

273   One can imagine a library requiring an extra copy of a work that is unobtainable. Its natural inclination would be to make the extra copy from one already in its possession. Such a case could reasonably arise with a book of local interest needed for reference and loan, or a work in fragile state, of which a photocopy could be lent more safely. To ensure against infringement of the law, that library would have to obtain a copy from another library instead of being allowed to make the copy itself. Even here, the Regulations possibly prevent this recourse, since copies may not be supplied to a library 'if a copy of that work or part has already been supplied to any person as a librarian of that library'. This can be read, though probably it was not intended, to include originally purchased printed copies of the

work, since the 'supply' mentioned in the Regulations is not limited
(e.g. as 'by any librarian') nor is 'copy' restricted to a product of the
act of copying as opposed to 'copies' of an edition. Again the problem
is one of the circumstances of libraries not being envisaged by either
the Gregory Committee or the drafters of the Regulations.

274 The effect of this interpretation would be that a library could supply
a copy of a work in its possession to a library that had no copy, but
not to a library that has one, unless it is damaged. The probable
intention of the Regulation is that a part of a work may be supplied to
make up a damaged copy, but the wording allows one to supply a
complete copy to a library with a damaged copy. Presumably
'damaged' need not mean 'incomplete' so a copy on crumbling paper
or with detached binding could be included. In the case of damaged
or faulty books or items, a library may wish to make up missing
sections, in a similar way. Here the protection would be adequate if the
part to be copied was less than substantial, but otherwise the same
rule applies — have it copied by another library.

275 It is hard to see any reasonable purpose in this condition, but a little
easier to divine its origin. This seems to have been the proposal to the
Gregory Committee by the Library Association on behalf of the
National Central Library that it, and other libraries when asked for a
loan copy of a book they are unwilling to remove even temporarily
from a reference collection, should be empowered to make up to a
complete copy to supply in lieu of a loan, either by microfilm or by
contact photography. The Gregory Committee's recommendation was
that this should be permitted provided the copyright owner agreed or
could not be traced. It seems probable that the eventuality of a library
wanting to copy for itself was not considered by the Gregory Committee
and therefore not provided for in its recommendations. The only
other reason one can think of is a general unwillingness to make
copying too easy and free from formalities.

276 **Can a library make a copy for a user, but lend it instead of sell it
to him?**
No. The attractive idea that a library can photocopy, say, an article
from a periodical instead of lending the part to a would-be borrower,
and cancel out the requirement to charge him by allowing him to
return it after use, is not permitted, since the recipient has to sign a
declaration that he will not use the copy except for purposes of research
or private study. It makes no difference whether the library subse-
quently uses the copy again, even if on the second or a subsequent
occasion it is permanently supplied. It has become by then an infringing
copy. Still less permissible is the occasional practice of academic
libraries of making a photocopy of an item, whether extract or article,

and storing it for future borrowing requirements. Reasonable alternatives would be the purchasing of extra copies or requesting permission.

277 What conditions attach to the use of copies acquired by libraries from other libraries?
None, provided the copy has been made according to the conditions of the Regulations. The copy received may be stored, lent, and, apparently, used for the making of further copies under the Regulations for supply to users, as well as being supplied directly to a user.

278 Can one make more than one copy of a permitted copy if they are supplied to different people?
Technically, yes. But the cautious librarian, especially one employed in an academic library, may query whether each one is required for the purposes of research or private study. Copies for class work are not to be included, whether at school or college, and it is extremely doubtful whether copies required by a teacher to be studied individually in private, e.g. 'homework' could be properly designated private study. Certainly the teacher cannot have them made together or even separately. The purpose of 'research' is not restricted to private research, so all members of a research team may be supplied with copies of the same item, provided they obtain them individually. A difficult borderline must be drawn in the case of committee or similar group work: this would not normally appear to be research, but members of a working party with a specific brief might well claim that their activity was research.

279 Must cash always change hands when copies are requested?
There are two problems here. The first concerns situations in which the passing of cash seems quite inappropriate, the the second where there is a logistical difficulty in making the transaction.

280 An extreme example of the first case could be that of a schoolchild assigned a specific part of a project, who discovers in the school reference library an essential item he needs to read at home. The school librarian could well be as unable to accept the cash as the child is unwilling or unable to pay. The exceptions for educational use of copyright works do not allow for this situation. There appears to be no solution, except to insist on payment.

281 In colleges and universities, the matter is less troublesome, since older students are more likely to have and to expect to spend cash on educational requisites. The tutors, and other staff, on the other hand, may well expect to have their research or private study needs funded by their employers, and may demand free copying from the library. If the institution is willing to fund the staff in this way, it should be by way of refund after cash payment has been made, or by some voucher system. The same conditions attach to other organisations: learned societies, government departments and the like.

282   This Regulation is almost certainly the one most frequently broken, and the law could not be said to have foreseen the circumstances of legitimate copies being made by libraries for institutional staff. The only possible benefit to copyright owners in these cases of adhering strictly to the rules is that of making the act of copying more administratively difficult. Though perhaps a worthy aim it is probably not what was intended by the legislators.

283   The second set of circumstances arises when users are at a distance from their libraries. A letter requesting the loan of a periodical part when only a reference copy is available, cannot be satisfied except by a photocopy, and without payment being agreed between library and user, that copy cannot be made. (There is the further difficulty about a declaration, for which see 262). The sensible solution is to telephone the user to confirm the acceptability of a photocopy, for which payment must be made, but this is not always possible, and can itself be a costly procedure.

284   **Can a user request a copy and sign a declaration on its receipt, e.g. by post?**
Legally, no, since the form of words relating to declarations states that no copy may be supplied to an individual 'unless he has delivered to the libraries concerned . . . a declaration and undertaking in writing . . . ' One can see the force of this insistence on the prior declaration, since copies may be made in good faith and received in bad. At that point it may be impossible to correct the wrong, and thereby protect the library. However, it is another of the aspects of the Regulations which is infringed very frequently, especially by libraries that serve their users at a distance, and it could well be said that the inconvenience to the user resulting from adhering to the Regulation is unreasonably great in comparison with the benefit to the copyright owner gained by obeying it.

285   **What obligations does a library have in keeping the declarations?**
No formal instructions have been laid down. Since an action for infringement of copyright can be taken up to six years after it occurred, the librarian needs to keep his collected declarations for seven years to make his record secure. A signed declaration would be a good defence for the library even if the copy turned out to be an infringement; provided, of course, that it could also be shown that the library acted in good faith, and within the Regulations. Otherwise there are no facilities in the law for inspection of declarations, nor is there any instruction on the order in which they should be filed.

286   Can photocopy charges be included in a general fee for miscellaneous services or a membership subscription?

Probably not, though there is little indication in the law. But such an arrangement would have copy charges part paid for by members or subscribers who had received none, thus subsidising those who had received them. A voucher system such as that operated by NRCd or BLLD is more acceptable since the charge for the voucher is directly related to the copies supplied. In the case of the BLLD, the basic form charge is for a loan or a minimum photocopy of 30 pages, coupons being added for lengthier copies.

287   What are the copyright implications of the BLLD photocopy service?

In many cases there is no difficulty, since copies are being supplied by one library to another. Payment is made by the prior charge for the form or by supplements in the form of photocopy coupons, and no declarations are required. But in the case of the BLLD supplying libraries that are not in the prescribed list of categories, or organisations that are not themselves libraries, the BLLD requires a statement that the copy is supplied for the purposes of research or private study, and since the library or office to which it supplies the copy is not qualified to make that declaration, the library or office is required to obtain a further declaration to that effect from the eventual user. The standard conditions of supply of forms to BLLD users require an undertaking that this procedure will be followed, and each form includes a brief declaration box. The BLLD does not, however, require the eventual users' declarations to be passed on to its office, and cannot therefore be completely satisfied that its copies have always been used for private study or research or supplied for the use of libraries of the prescribed types.

288   If a publisher of a book or periodical prints a warning notice prohibiting copying what power does this have?

It cannot over-ride the exceptions provided by the 1956 Act and Regulations. It does not alter the fact that only copying a substantial part is an infringement, even if the notices say 'no part' may be copied. Nor does it affect the right of the private student or researcher to take copies for his own use, nor that of the library to supply copies under certain conditions. But it would be reasonable to suppose that publishers using such warning notices are not parties to the 'general licence' offered by the Publishers Association and the Society of Authors in *Photocopying and the law*, or at least not in the publication in question. It could be inviting protests for a library to invoke the 'general licence' to extend its copying power beyond the Section 7 powers in such cases.

289   If a periodical publisher charges a higher subscription price to libraries, does that give libraries the right to copy more freely?

No, but some periodical publishers do at the same time offer copying licences, in exchange for a percentage surcharge (sometimes 30% has been mentioned). This may give the library permission to copy a limited amount (e.g. up to 10 copies of any one article) or it may give complete freedom to copy within the library. Anything savouring of re-publishing would need to be separately negotiated. Such schemes have not so far gained much popularity in this country, probably because libraries find they can manage to serve their users without recourse to special licences.

290   In special libraries, information scientists or librarians frequently need to build up briefing files on topics likely to be investigated by their colleagues in the near future. Photocopies of articles form an important part of such files. Can they be made legally?
Not very readily. In such cases, the librarian may discover the required article either by seeing it in a periodical the library receives, or by finding an index or abstract entry in a secondary source. In the latter case he can legitimately request a copy from another library, and this can then be filed against the time it may be needed. But in the case of a journal the library receives, the following appear to be the possible legitimate choices:

(a) tear out the article and file it
(b) list a reference to the article in the file
(c) ask the author or publisher for an off-print or tear sheet
(d) request permission to photocopy
(e) buy another copy of the issue.

In the case of (b) a photocopy could be bought from another library should the periodical be discarded, but no photocopy from the library's own copy should be made until the researcher or other user actually requests it.

291   The only reasonable solution to this problem is for the library to seek a general licence from the publisher of its most frequently demanded periodicals to take copies for briefing files, unless the publisher is ready to supply off-prints of all articles. This is unlikely, since the practice of supplying off-prints is dwindling, and in any case their main purpose is for direct communication between author and researcher. They are therefore supplied to the authors, and stocks are less frequently held by the publisher. A principal reason for the diminishing popularity of off-prints must undoubtedly be the increase of photocopying.

292   What is the copyright position of abstracts?
There are several problems or queries in dealing with abstracts. They involve creating abstracts, reprinting other people's abstracts, and copying abstracts. Unfortunately there is little in the way of commentary on the subject to guide us. In the matter of creating

abstracts, librarians are frequently in the position of circulating current awareness bulletins and may need to compile abstracts of articles or other works. This they are perfectly entitled to do, provided the product of their work is indeed an abstract and does not substitute for the original. A further protection for copying or summarising news items exists in the special exception under Section 6 of the Act for fair dealing for the purpose of reporting current events. Obviously a scientific periodical article is very rarely to do with current events in the sense of general news, so summarising must be brief. The reproduction of key tables, formulae, arguments and extended conclusions might very well not be regarded as a fair summary. As frequently happens, periodical articles may be supplied by the author or editor with their own abstracts. Although I have not seen it argued or stated, it is the general practice for author abstracts to be regarded as common property. Librarians freely include them in their bulletins, and indeed frequently shorten or amend them.

293 The formal publication of abstract journals depends therefore on these two freedoms: to summarise articles and papers, and to reproduce abstracts prepared by the journals themselves. The service provided by the abstract journals in collecting abstracts from a wide variety of sources, arranging and indexing them, is regarded tacitly as sufficient payment for the privilege of redistributing the product of original work. Once an abstracts periodical has been published, however, it is protected from copying as an original work itself. Obviously, to copy one or two abstracts is not taking a substantial part, whether for republication or merely photocopying. The argument that each abstract is a unit, and that to take a complete abstract would be a substantial part and therefore an infringement could be sustained, but the lack of complete originality in an abstract would be a defence against the argument.

294 If one asks what constitutes an 'article' in an abstracts journal that could be copied under Section 7 of the Act and the Libraries Regulations, it would be difficult to say. Common sense seems to be called for rather than a fine legal definition. A photocopy of up to 10% of an issue of an abstracts journal might seem fair, but if that constitutes a complete section and if one then copies the same complete section for each issue of a volume (or even of several or all volumes), one could have a bibliography of a self-contained subject. Such a practice, which could then ramify into supplying other sections on a regular basis to other users, would seem to be in positive competition with the original. The repetitive nature of abstracts journals leads one to suggest a different interpretation of the 'any one article' rule. A complete section might be permitted for copying on one occasion, but regular copying should probably be more restricted — below the 10% level or the extent of a complete section. The Act defines 'article' as

an item of any description: this could presumably refer either to a
single abstract or a self-contained section. Once again one can offer
little authoritative guidance because the drafters of the Act have failed
to foresee the problem, and even the spirit of the Act in unclear in its
operation here. What one can say for certain is that reproduction in
other publications, whether internal library bulletins or more generally
available media, of sections of abstracts of any length, cannot be done
without permission, since it is not private study, and not for reporting
current news or events, and is definitely multiple copying. Of course,
by coincidence one might come to the same result in a library bulletin
by reproducing abstracts from individual articles as is reached by a
formally published abstracts journal. But if one could demonstrate
how one arrived at the result, it is unlikely that the abstracts journal
could hold the library bulletin had copied it, unless some tell-tale sign
were present such as the abstracts journal's notation, arrangement,
typography, subject headings or verbal modifications to the original.

295   Is Cataloguing in Publication (CIP) data copyright?
Officially, yes, but the British Library, which holds the copyright, is
unlikely to consider any action using CIP data as an infringement,
unless — most improbably — the data is taken from a large quantity of
books to build up into a publication that is colourably like the British
National Bibliography. One can therefore use the CIP data from
books added to one's library to create one's own catalogue records, or
input to one's library accessions lists, without fear of protest from
the British Library.

296   May one copy illustrations from books and periodicals?
Illustrations count as artistic works, and each one has its own copyright
protection as a separate work. This is the case whether the illustration
is an artistic engraving or a geometrical diagram. To copy the whole
of an illustration can therefore be an infringement as copying a
substantial part, i.e. all, of an individual item. Certainly to copy all
or most of the illustrations in a book which is published principally
to exhibit those illustrations would be an infringement. There are
cases, however, where illustrations can be copied: under the Libraries
Regulations, any or all of the illustrations accompanying an article
can be copied: this would be the case even in an art magazine when
an article consisted only of illustrations with captions. There is less
freedom in books, but if a textual extract is a reasonable part and if
the other conditions are fulfilled, any or all illustrations that accompany
that extract may be copied. Thus it may be possible to argue that a
certain number of illustrations may not be copied on their own, but if
the accompanying text is copied as well, then the copying is legal.
Before one objects to this as nonsense, it is as well to remember that
a 'reasonable part' is copiable only under the Regulations, which
require application to the copyright owner if traceable, while copying

of less than a substantial part, which is permitted to anyone, could well never include any illustrations.

297 The 'general licence' in *Photocopying and the law* is extended also to illustrations in books and peridicals, so the extra facilities offered, e.g. to non-prescribed libraries, and in setting out safe maximum copying proportions, can be applied also to illustrations. But the licence offers no modification of the principle of considering each individual illustration as a work bearing copyright.

298 **How far can libraries copy music scores?**
The basic principles of the law apply equally to music as to literary and dramatic works, but it is worth noting that there is no definition available of a musical work. No copying of less than a substantial part will be an infringement, but it must be remembered that even a short theme has been held a substantial part. One problem encountered more frequently with music than other literature is the absence of dates of publication, making it more difficult to establish whether items are in copyright. A further problem is the frequency of arrangements which will carry copyright separate from that of the original music. And of course any words set to the music have a separate copyright. It would seem that a complete piece of music may be copied under the Libraries Regulations if it appears in an issue of a periodical, since by definition 'article' is an item of any description. Music in collections is copiable only under the same conditions as excerpts from books; if a substantial part is required, copying without permission is provided for libraries only if the copyright owner is untraceable after reasonable enquiry.

299 The Code of fair practice issued by the Music Publishers Association (ref. 10a), helps only slightly to ease libraries' difficulties. For study and research (it need not be private study, apparently), short excerpts may be copied, but a short excerpt is defined as 'less than a perform-able unit of music.' One supposes that such excerpts would not amount to substantial parts either, in many cases. Libraries are, however, implicitly allowed under this Code to act for users in other circumstances, and this means that in emergencies, for example, such as those described, libraries could legitimately make copies for performances when requested. The conditions of these permissions are set out more fully later (539-40). This Code applies only, however, to works copyrighted by any of a list of copyright owners given as an appendix to the Code. The Music Publishers Association is willing to help in tracing copyright owners' and publishers' whereabouts in other cases.

3
Background to the Copyright Act 1956

301 At the end of the Second World War the scholarly world emerged to pick up the threads of its activities, operating, so far as the copying of published and unpublished materials went, under the Copyright Act of 1911. In that Act the concept of 'fair dealing' was available as a protection to those who copied out parts of books or journals for the purposes of research or private study. No mention was made of libraries in this context, probably because they were mostly in no position to offer facilities to their users to copy printed matter. The student's protection was from infringement in the copying out of extracts by hand or typewriter. Fast copying machinery other than straightforward photography was unknown in 1911, and libraries offered little in the way of photographic services. However, by 1945, the scientific community in particular was in grave need of fast access to published material, much of it in journals, and had gone some way by means of microphotography and contact photography, to make copying technically a little easier.

Royal Society Conference

302 In 1948 the Royal Society held a major Scientific Information Conference, to discuss possible improvements in the production, abstracting, indexing and distribution of scientific literature. Among its recommendations the following appeared under the heading of 'Provision of separates and copies':

"The Conference considers the ready availability of separates and copies of papers and abstracts, of great importance. The current practice whereby reprints are obtained on application to the author has great value in promoting the personal contacts which result from individual exchanges, but the conference concludes that increased facililties are required . . .

"The Royal Society is invited to exert its influence to obtain universal acceptance of the following principle:

Science rests upon its published record, and ready access to published scientific and technical information is a fundamental need of scientists everywhere. All bars which prevent access to scientific and technical publications hinder the progress of science and should be removed.

"Making single copies of extracts from books or periodicals is essential to research workers, and the production of such single extract copies, by or on behalf of scientists, is necessary for scientific practice".

Under the heading 'Library and information services', it is recommended:

"The Conference has concluded that libraries have a special responsibility in facilitating the distribution of separates, and copies of papers and abstracts." (ref. 39.)

Fair Copying Declaration

303 Following the Conference the Royal Society's Information Service Committee produced in 1950 a Fair Copying Declaration on fair dealing in regard to copying from scientific periodicals. This was accompanied by lists of signatories and of the journals they published, which were to be covered. The declaration stated that it would be regarded by the signatories as fair dealing when non-profit organisations such as libraries, archives, museums or information services made and delivered single copies of part of a periodical issue to a user who set out in writing that he required it for private study, research, criticism or review, and that he would not sell it or reproduce it for publication. Further conditions warned the recipient about misuse, required the copy to be made without profit to the maker, proper acknowledgement of the source of the copy, and that only one copy be made for any one person. The 1950 issue of the *Declaration* listed 118 organisations, the second edition in 1952 131 organisations, and the third edition in 1957 143 organisations. The third edition appeared after the Copyright Act 1956 but before the Regulations (1957) came into force. (ref. 38.)

Gregory Committee

304 In 1948 the Berne Convention on Copyright was revised at Brussels and the President of the Board of Trade set up a committee in 1951 to examine the implications for the U.K. of becoming a signatory. This was the Gregory Committee. Apart from the Berne Convention revision they were instructed to consider 'technical developments'. After 18 months (April 1951 to October 1952) the report was published. (ref. 36.) Following an introductory section the first matter to be considered was Term of copyright — the 1911 Act had contained a statutory licence to republish in the second 25 years of an author's copyright after death and this was at odds with the new Berne Convention text — but the second subject was 'fair dealing'. The Gregory Committee considered the most important matter under this heading was copying by photographic means. They saw three distinct aspects: copying periodical literature, copying books, and copying manuscripts, and they thought they presented different problems. They stated first that anything that could be considered fair dealing, if done by a student himself, should also be fair dealing if done for him by a librarian.

305   In periodical copying the Committee followed the path lit for them by the Royal Society. With a little modification, they thought, the Royal Society's arrangements could be extended to cover all periodical publications. The conditions for operating the copying arrangements should be prescribed by statutory order, which could be revised from time to time in the light of experience. The six elements the Committee specified as necessary to be included were all featured in the Royal Society's *Declaration*. They covered the non-profit making status of the library making the copy; the research or private study purpose for the copy; only one copy to be made; only one article to be copied (and that the copy does not constitute substantially the whole issue); the need to charge not less than the cost price (with an allowance for overheads); the provision of an undertaking by the recipient concerning the purpose of the copy.

306   Book copying raised two problems: that of copying extracts for students, and of copying the whole book where it was out of print and was needed through the interlending system. The evidence of the Library Association, influenced heavily by the practices of the National Central Library, pressed for this latter facility. The Committee felt that there was unlikely to be the same urgency to make copies as in the case of periodical articles, and that the Library Association and others had not made out a case for copying substantial parts without seeking permission. The Committee therefore recommended that Libraries should be allowed to make copies, again under set regulations, but only after attempts to gain copyright permission had failed through inability to contact the copyright owner.

307   The matter of copying from manuscripts was then considered by the Committee, and they came to the conclusion, largely reflected in the Copyright Act 1956, that copies could be made for private purposes at the end of certain periods — 50 years after the author's death and 100 years after the making of the manuscript. The Committee recognised that the copyright owner was sometimes not the same person or persons as the owner of the manuscripts, and that manuscripts deposited in libraries with no restrictions attached could still be subject to the control of a different copyright owner.

308   After some consideration of legal deposit, on which the Committee made a few minor suggestions, the main bulk of the Gregory

Committee's report consists of two Parts; the first on gramophone records, films, broadcast performances, sporting spectacles and performances of artistes, and the second on performing and performers' rights. Some consideration of these matters will be given in the later chapter on audio-visual materials.

309 As far as libraries are concerned, therefore, the Gregory Committee's Report had a large influence on the shaping of the relevant sections in the Copyright Act 1956. Indeed some of the provisions of the Act are more intelligible when read in the light of the Report, though of course the Report cannot be used as an official interpretation of the Act. Indeed some of the Committee's recommendations were not taken up by the Parliamentary draughtsmen, and some new provisions were added during the Bill's passage through Parliament.

4
Developments from the Copyright Act 1956 to 1973

401 The previous chapter traced some of the episodes in the history of copyright leading up to the Copyright Act. The present chapter takes that story further, detailing what was said and written about the Act as it applied to library matters, from its coming into force to the setting up, 17 years later, of the Whitford Committee. Several of the publications to be considered have influenced interpretations of the law as set out in the earlier chapter of questions and answers.

R. Staveley : The reader, the writer and copyright law

402 Very soon after the Act was passed, and indeed before it came into force (1st June 1957) or the Regulations had been drafted, Ronald Staveley, of University College, London, gave a lecture on the implications of the new Act. (ref. 15). In it he first reminds us that the Act became law only after an earlier Bill, based on the Gregory Report, had been withdrawn, and after a dissolution of Parliament. After noting the influence on it of international agreements he emphasises the position of manuscripts in library collections, and then remarks that copying apparatus found in libraries is 'capable of minor publishing work', and that the Act limits the librarian's freedom in copying in comparison with the individual scholar or researcher. Staveley also says that though librarians' provisions for photocopying are less generous in the Act than had been hoped for, they are less restrictive than for example in West Germany.

G. Woledge : Copyright and libraries in the United Kingdom

403 In June 1958 the *Journal of documentation* published a paper by G. Woledge, Librarian of the British Library of Political and Economic Science at the L.S.E. (ref. 19). In this paper Woledge discusses the background to the Act and what its provisions mean for Librarians. It is an excellently clear piece of writing and has had considerable influence, together with a later article that I shall come to in due course. However, the first note of controversy is sounded by Woledge's insistence that what is forbidden the librarian under Section 7 of the Act may be permitted him under Section 6 by the subsection (1) that allows 'fair dealing' for purposes of research or private study. This matter was discussed earlier (228-36). Other matters dealt with in Woledge's paper are the provision for typographic arrangement protection, and its poor drafting; the seven situations (including 'fair dealing' and the libraries' regulations) in which copying can legally be done. He goes on to explain the libraries' regulations, in some detail, mentions translations briefly, and concludes that for librarians the 'new library exemptions probably authorise little if anything more than was already allowed'.

Criticism and review

404   In the same year, 1958, the Society of Authors and the Publishers Association issued a joint statement on reproduction for purposes of criticism or review. In it they set out what they regarded as limits up to which no reasonable objection could be taken. These 'fair dealing' quotations could be up to 400 words for a single extract, or a series of quotations up to a total of 800 words of which no single extract exceeds 300 words. This is for prose: for poetry an extract or extracts can total 40 lines, but is not to exceed one quarter of any poem. Greater latitude would be allowed for newly published work. These permissions should not be used for compiling anthologies.

Photocopying and the law

405   Seven years later the same two organisations produced a lengthier pamphlet designed to deal with reasonable limits of photocopying. *Photocopying and the law*, published in 1965 by the Society of Authors and the Publishers Association, and subtitled 'a guide for librarians and teachers and other suppliers and users of photocopies of copyright works', (ref. 14) has as its main purpose the definition of the length of extracts that the two bodies regard as not amounting to a substantial part of a work, which could then be photocopied without need to apply for permission to the copyright owners. Harking back to the criticism and review quantities they multiplied them by ten, so that a single copy of an extract may be made up to 4,000 words, or a series of extracts up to a total of 8,000 words, provided no single extract is more than 3,000 words. A further proviso is that the total amount copied must not exceed 10% of the whole work. Individual poems, essays and other short literary works cannot be regarded as copiable parts of the books in which they appear.

406   The two bodies say that their permissions may be used by librarians of any type of library, whether conducted for profit or not, but other conditions laid down by the libraries Regulations should, they say,

be observed, such as obtaining suitable declarations from the recipients of the copies.

407 It has been insufficiently noticed, however, that through an unfortunate choice of terms, this pamphlet, while reassuring librarians of what may safely be done, at the same time adds confusion to the scene. In offering these limits of what may be copied from non-periodical works before permission needs to be sought, the Society of Authors and Publishers Association employed the term 'fair dealing', whereas in fact they were offering a definition of what can be copied before a substantial part is taken. As D. C. Pearce puts it: 'Fair dealing is concerned with the use that is going to be made of the reproduction and is a distinct issue from the question whether a substantial portion of the work is reproduced. It is only if the whole or a substantial part of the work is reproduced that the question of fair dealing can arise.' (ref. 150.)

408 *Photocopying and the law* goes on to deal with illustrations. Recognising that single illustrations unaccompanied by text are required for projection use in education, they say no objection is made to single copy copying of illustrative material (whether as photo-positive or slides), provided it is used solely in a school or other educational establishment. The Society of Authors and Publishers Association then deal with multiple copies. The burden of this section is that permission must always be sought, except of course where the law (Section 41 again) allows it, in setting examination questions.

G. Woledge : Copyright and library photocopying

409 In July 1967, G. Woledge published a follow-up article (ref. 20) to his 1958 piece (ref. 19). In it he deals with individual cases that bother librarians and offers solutions. He repeats his view that the 'fair dealing' protection offered by Section 6 is available to librarians when copying for research or private study, suggests that a 'not substantial' defence could be offered against a charge that typographical arrangement copyright is infringed by photocopying under Section 6, welcomes the 'general licence' of the Society of Authors and Publishers Association, notes the facility for interlibrary copying, and suggests self-service copiers should be provided for copying only to the extent that the library would copy for the user. He suggests that multiple copy copying could be permitted under Section 6, if the purposes of research or private study were being served, but not in an educational institution, where it is expressly forbidden by Section 41. He concludes by saying that though some uses of photography, especially those not under the control of scrupulous persons, may be detrimental to the interests of copyright owners, the general encouragement to the use of literature that xerography offers will in the long run be beneficial to the producers of books. There is an appendix, in which he argues his case against the S. of A. and P.A.'s view that 'fair dealing' copying can only be done by an individual (see chapter 2, 230-4).

British Copyright Council

410   In 1970 *Photocopying and the law* was taken over and re-issued in a revised text by the British Copyright Council, a body representative of a number of authors' and book trade organisations. The quantitative recommendations of the pamphlet were untouched, but a few changes in wording were made. One of them, concerning the 'fair dealing' argument, replaces the phrase 'legal precedent, however, has established that such 'fair dealing' must be exercised by the individual for himself' with 'There is, however, some authority for holding that such 'fair dealing'. . . '; a change that probably takes account of Woledge's note in his 1967 article.

R. E. Barker : Photocopying practices in the United Kingdom

411   Also in 1970, R. E. Barker, Secretary of the Publishers Association, and architect of the *Photocopying and the law* general licence, published the results of a survey among 400 libraries in 1967, (ref. 21). Prefixed to the study is a consideration of the law. No new interpretations are offered, but there is a softening of the line against libraries being permitted to shelter under the 'fair dealing' exception of Section 6(1). With the law so uncertain, Barker says, 'conscientious compromises of this sort are doubtless inevitable', and in his 'Summary of the law as interpreted' he goes so far as to include the 'fair dealing' option as one of the five ways in which libraries may make single copy photocopies. Barker rejects, however, the idea, tentatively put forward by Woledge, that multiple copying might be permissible if it is for research or private study, by bringing in the effect of multiple distribution on the original work.

412   In the study of then current copying practices, Barker reports that the distinction between the libraries prescribed by the Act and Regulations and other libraries was unclear and should be abandoned since only copying that is itself for profit would have any effect on the copyright owner's interests. Commercial copying agencies, on the other hand, should pay a percentage of their receipts to a central fund, and Barker thinks copying equipment could also be subject to a levy. In commenting on the survey of copying then being done, Barker believes he sees evidence that while the taking of multiple subscriptions to journals may make for less copying in a library, multiple book provision has no such effect. Most of the copying done could be authorised by changing the law in respect of for-profit libraries and by adopting the 'general licence' of *Photocopying and the law* into the legislation. Payments for copying that fell outside these provisions could be made to a central

authority at a set rate. Whether the user should be charged could be left to individual libraries. He then goes on to discuss the type of arrangements needed for such a body. The level of payments he thinks needs to be widely discussed, and should be subject to review when agreed.

Principles of photocopying

413 Barker concludes his study with a Postscript on the photocopying arrangements agreed for recommendation to individual countries by an International Committee of Experts meeting in Paris in July 1968. Here the intention was to advise national legislators on what should reasonably be permitted. Barker identifies 10 principles:

(1) all processes analogous to photography are treated as such

(2) personal use copying should be permitted

(3) non profit libraries should be permitted to make single copies for each user, of single articles or reasonable extracts

(4) unpublished works in libraries may be copied only by copyright permission

(5) microform copies for conservation in non-profit libraries should be permitted

(6) libraries should be allowed to make full-size duplicates for preserving their collections after ensuring that sale copies are not available

(7) pages may be copied to make up imperfect copies in non-profit library collections

(8) such copies in (7) may be supplied by other libraries

(9) copies may be made by non-profit libraries within the framework of licence agreements

(10) educational use copies may be made for non-profit schools etc. for use by teachers and students.

414 While giving his support to measures designed to ease the procedures for scholars and librarians to make legitimate photocopies, Barker emphasises that with the increasing use of microforms and full-size photocopies, and with likely further technical developments, the increasing number of physical forms in which an author's work is likely to be reproduced; certain kinds of work would eventually not be published in conventional printed form at all. The rewards of authorship could decline dramatically if the economics of authorship and publishing are not adjusted to allow for these new situations.

C. H. Gibbs Smith : Copyright law concerning works of art, etc.

415 A most succinct, accurate, useful and yet lively aid to those confronted by copyright problems is C. H. Gibbs Smith's 12 page pamphlet (ref. 10), principally written for museum curators, but of value to librarians and many others, which was first issued by the Museums Association in 1970, a revised edition being put out in 1974. Its special value for this study is in its treatment of artistic works, and it will be considered in more detail later.

Education

416 A digest on Copyright, published for teachers by the periodical *Education* (ref. 68) deals in a series of questions and answers with the situations both of the teacher as producer and user of copyright material. The former section, though the shorter, may well have more value for librarians since the latter mostly covers ground gone over more thoroughly elsewhere.

Copyright and education

417 An organisation having an equal interest in copyright but from a different angle is the Council for Educational Technology, formed to promote the use of technical methods in education. Under its earlier name, the National Council for Educational Technology issued a booklet in 1972 with the title *Copyright and education* (ref. 11). The concern of the CET is with the use of copyright materials in schools and other educational establishments, but the pamphlet takes a general view of the copyright position, beginning with an exposition of the present state of the law. As far as non-print materials are concerned, their discussion will be considered in chapter 7. Here we concentrate in the CET's treatment of print. After setting out the nature of rights that are protected, CET discusses exceptions, beginning with fair dealing. The provision that only copying a substantial part of a work can be an infringement is noted with the warning that even small parts can be significant and therefore 'substantial'.

418 Research and private study, CET next states, 'have been interpreted quite strictly', and it mentions the ruling on circulation of copies among students being an infringement. 'Private study', it says, cannot be extended to mean 'private use'. Under 'photocopying', CET merely mentions Section 7 of the Act, its attendant Regulations, and the pamphlet *Photocopying and the law*.

419 Then follows a section on educational use. It is pointed out that only primary and secondary schools come under the definition of the word 'school' in the Copyright Act 1956. CET also makes the point that while it is permitted the teacher to write texts on a blackboard or dictate them to people to write down, he may not save time and energy by distributing copies amongst them; at least not without applying for permission and possibly having to pay a fee. The examination questions and answers exception is noted with the comment that publication of extracts in these formats would not automatically be permitted. CET points to another oddity in that whereas literary, dramatic or musical works may be performed in schools only if the 'audience' is confined virtually to teachers and pupils, sound recordings may be played to a wider audience in schools provided no charge is made for admission.

Multiple copies

420   On multiple copies, CET comes out with a flat statement that they may be made by teachers only with copyright permission. However this generalisation is immediately qualified by the implication that 'a few copies of a passage for immediate use' may be made under the fair dealing provision. This is contrasted with the requirement to seek permission for complete works or substantial portions, and the remark that the action is usually planned rather than 'immediate' and there is therefore time to request permissions. There seems to be a contradiction or confusion here, since copying that is not substantial requires no 'fair dealing' defence: it stands on its own merits.

421   Most of the remainder of this section of *Copyright and education* is concerned with non-print materials, and will be discussed in chapter 7. But there is a reminder about separate copyright in artistic works; even though they may be only diagrams, graphs or statistical tables, they may contain the core of a work. A warning, too, is given about complications that can arise in music with different copyrights vesting in words, music, translations and arrangements.

422   Part I of *Copyright and education* ends with a resumé of what needs to be done, from the teachers' viewpoint, to improve matters. CET offers three possible courses of action. First, amendment of the Copyright Act 1956 (which will, it says, have to be revised if Britain is to sign the 1971 text of the Universal Copyright Convention) to allow wider educational copying facilities. This would, says CET, offend copyright holders. A second possible course would be to include a right to copy in the sale price of copyright material to educational institutions. The third possibility is one which CET specially favours; the development of agreements between copyright holders and groups of users. CET concludes with the observation that copyright owners cannot and should not be expected always to be charitable to educational users, and it offers its services in promoting an easier flow of ideas on the subject between owners and users so that less cumbersome arrangements can be arrived at.

Copying of print materials in schools

423   Before going on to consider the Whitford Committee and its Report, one other item needs considering. Although its report was not published until January 1975 (ref. 67), nearly a year after the Whitford Committee was set up, the Publishers Association's survey of the copying of print materials in schools was carried out in late 1973. The survey took place over seven weeks and at 17 primary and 49 secondary schools.

424   By extrapolation from the survey findings it was estimated that in a

school year about 108 million copies from publications (excluding periodicals and examination papers) might be made. This figure was reckoned to be a small percentage of school copying, the remainder being of material originating in the school. The survey report noted that of the titles copied one third were 'course books', themselves designed for multiple use in schools, but of the total number of copies produced, 'course books' represented 46%. The survey report carried a foreword in which it was hoped that the evidence produced would help the concerned parties to come to 'some arrangement under which reasonable copying by schools might be done with reasonable safeguards (and perhaps some reward) to authors and other copyright proprietors'.

Legal commentaries

425   No mention has been made of legal texts on copyright to date. In the main, such works as Copinger and Skone James (ref. 3), Eddy (ref. 8), Cavendish or Whale (ref. 18) have little to add to the interpretations we have been looking at in this chapter, though the fullest study, Copinger and Skone James, is the original exposition on which some of the interpretations we have looked at have been based. It is worth noting that no case has yet been made arising from the Copyright Act 1956 that concerns the actions of libraries or librarians. Consequently the three editions of Copinger and Skone James that have appeared since 1956 (the 9th, 1958, 10th 1965, and 11th 1971) carry substantially the same text on matters affecting libraries.

5
The Whitford Committee and its Report

501 This chapter considers the move to set up the Whitford Committee; some of the evidence submitted to it; the Committee's proposals on Reprography and some general matters, such as ownership and length of copyright; and some of the reactions to the Report that have been made public.

502 The Whitford Committee's brief was to review the law of copyright with specific attention to current technology facilitating copying of print and sound records and tapes; and the working of the Design Copyright Act of 1968. The committee was specifically instructed not to give any consideration to the matter of public lending right. The committee was chaired by Mr. Justice Whitford, and included Mr. E. P. Skone James, the Middle Temple barrister noted for his work on Copinger and Skone James on Copyright, for the 11th edition of which he was completely responsible (ref. 3). It took time for the Committee to get under weigh. An announcement made in August 1973 that the Committee would be set up was not implemented until February 1974. The Committee reported in March 1977 having taken written evidence from 267 individuals and organisations (200 organisations having been directly approached by the Committee), and oral evidence from 66 individuals and organisations. Neither written nor oral evidence was published by the Committee, though those who submitted it were free to do so, and in many cases did. We shall look at evidence submitted by 11 bodies: The Library Association, Aslib, the Standing Conference of National and University Libraries, the Institute of Information Scientists, the British Council, the Council for Educational Technology, the Inner London Education Authority, the British Copyright Council, the British Printing Industries Federation, the Publishers Association, and the Association of Learned and Professional Society Publishers.

Evidence to the Whitford Committee
The Library Association

503 The Library Association's evidence made the following points:

(1) the making of single extract copies from books and periodicals is essential for the purposive use of all literature
(2) four principles should be adhered to in controlling copyright material in libraries:
   (a) authors and publishers should be protected against unfair copying in libraries
   (b) information should be widely available
   (c) laws and regulations should be enforceable
   (d) the minimum of time and effort should be needed to secure permissions
(3) fair dealing should be clarified
(4) the libraries' exceptions are restrictive
(5) wider powers for libraries in copying can be justified by the greater control that library copying exercises compared with copying elsewhere in institutions; there is no evidence that journal article copying harms sales
(6) a proposal is made that 'fair dealing' exceptions should apply to libraries; limits should be specified
(7) a further proposal is that all types of library should be admitted to the libraries exceptions, and that extensions to a library's copying powers be made:
   (a) to make an extra copy for library stock
   (b) to complete an existing damaged copy in its possession
   (c) to dispense with individual declarations, and substitute overall declarations by each library user
   (d) method and amount of payment for copies to be left to libraries' discretion
   (e) permission to make one copy of an out of print book that has been unavailable for the past three years and is not planned for reissue within the next three years
(8) licensing should be introduced for copying above these levels
(9) educational performance exceptions allowed in Section 41 of the 1956 Act should be extended to library premises
(10) audio visual materials require special provision, and licensing arrangements for educational use should be completed by the C.E.T.; in addition:
   (a) the fair dealing concept should be brought in
   (b) educational exceptions should be extended to colleges and universities and their libraries
   (c) licences should be 'blanket' in operation, cutting out the need to obtain permissions
   (d) 'fair dealing' for libraries could help to control unfair use by individuals and teachers
(11) microforms require some special provisions:
   (a) enlargement from and duplication of microforms are to be recognised as the making of a copy, as well as producing the original microform
   (b) copying one text or a substantial part of one text should constitute an infringement of copyright on a microform containing more than one text
   (c) blanket licensing should be introduced for microform duplicating machines
(12) legal deposit should be extended to non-book materials, in particular:
   (a) films and videotapes
   (b) filmstrips and loops
   (c) sound recordings
   (d) microforms
(13) no change is proposed on the law relating to archives.

504 This evidence was submitted in July 1974, and in June 1975 oral evidence was given by the Library Association's Copyright sub-committee. Points that arose in dicussion included the effects of photocopying on periodical publishing, the principle and means of operating a blanket licence for library copying, personal and corporate responsibility for keeping to the law, the place of commercial and industrial libraries, legal deposit of non-book materials, and copyright in unpublished documents. The only change of viewpoint presented by the L.A. was a suggestion that perpetual copyright should not subsist in unpublished documents held in open library collections. The Whitford Committee invited the L.A. to submit supplementary evidence on the idea of blanket licensing. This was done, but no modification of view was put forward. Instead the L.A. re-emphasised its view that it saw no reason why libraries should not continue to be allowed to make single extract copies without payment of fees. Blanket licensing would be appropriate for multiple copying, and for machines not under the library's control.

Aslib

505 Aslib's proposed submission was the subject of a half-day symposium. The points Aslib wished to make were:

(1) librarians conscientiously avoided copyright infringement
(2) priorities for libraries in copying were:
    (a) avoidance of delay in satisfying users
    (b) minimum of administrative procedures
    (c) payments should be low, openly arrived at, and methods of payment simple
(3) general principles for libraries to conform to voluntarily should be promulgated
(4) endorse the Royal Society's fair copying declaration, and the Libraries Regulations, except for the restrictions on for-profit libraries, which should be lifted; microfilming for storage purposes should be permitted under the Regulations
(5) tariffs for multiple copying should be promulgated, with a simple mechanism for passing the fee on to the copyright owner
(6) permissions should be sought for copying in excess of stated maxima
(7) publicly funded work should not attract further rewards for the author through copyright payments
(8) copyright duration in periodical publications should be examined, and could reasonably terminate six months after publication where copies are no longer in print
(9) copyright in secondary publications (abstracts, indexes, etc.) should have a clearly recognised copyright, and should be free from the risk of infringement of copyright of the primary publication on which they are based.

Standing Conference of National and University Libraries

506 SCONUL made the following points:

(1) the Royal Society declaration (303) was endorsed and should be extended to all academic and research activity

(2) the interdependence of scholarly libraries, publishers and authors was stressed, and the importance of reasonable access for users to published writings

(3) the principles of individual responsibility and fair dealing were the foundations of SCONUL's evidence

(4) copying infringements should be the responsibility of the individual, hence the undesirability of requiring a librarian to obtain a declaration from the user. Instead, libraries should display prominent notices about compliance with copyright law

(5) if individuals are made responsible for copying, the Libraries Regulations will be unnecessary, since libraries will be acting only as agents, though library copying for reference purposes will need to be provided for

(6) special conditions, such as minimum charges to users, should be removed, and thus recognise the present position where institutions bear all costs for their members

(7) fair dealing should be given greater emphasis and be further clarified: copying a book that has been out of print for a reasonable period of time and is not scheduled for reprinting should be recognised as fair dealing

(8) multiple copying can be fair dealing when short extracts are required for teaching or group study

(9) legal deposit requires no amendment for printed works, but its application should be more effective

(10) fair dealing and individual responsibility principles should also apply to non-book materials

(11) the CET's negotiations for licensing non-book material use should make access for study purposes easier

(12) surcharges on recording equipment should not be introduced

(13) BBC non-educational broadcasts should be permitted to be copied as educational ones. The requirement to erase them after one year should be re-examined

(14) legal deposit arrangements should be brought in for microforms, records, films, audio-tapes, videotapes and related materials, and national archives maintained of such material

(15) these recommendations are made to facilitate the use of books and non-book materials for teaching and learning, not to avoid purchasing them or deprive creators of their rewards.

Institute of Information Scientists

507 The Institute's submission makes the following points:

(1) support for the L.A. and Aslib's submissions

(2) monopoly of copyright should carry the obligation to make the information in the protected work available to the public; a comparison with patent law is made

(3) copies should be permissible without reference to the publisher, provided they are not sold by way of trade

(4) whole or substantially whole works should be copiable if they are unavailable for purchase

(5) there is frequently no time to seek permission to copy

(6) a new law should define types of publication and prescribe regulations for each: fiction, music, etc. should be separated from scientific and technical titles

(7) the user's needs should be considered in the case of scientific and technical literature, and the importance of fast access to it

(8) characteristics of scientific and technical literature include the

absence of profit to the author, the reliance of its publisher on
advertising revenue, its purpose to spread information quickly, the
short period in which it is in print

(9)   books are different from journals: the former are frequently
updated, the latter never; copyright abuse can harm the former, not
the latter

(10) the copyright protection of secondary publications is stressed in the
same terms as in Aslib's submission

(11) translations of periodical articles should not require copyright
permission

(12) microform and other storage copies should be permitted to be made
by the owner of a copy of the original without copyright permission

(13) typographic arrangement copyright should be modified: the 25 year
period is excessive, and something between five and ten years
substituted; modifications to the coming into force of typographic
copyright are also suggested.

British Council

508 The Council asks for two modifications of the law in its submission:

(1)   removal of the need to charge for copies supplied: in the Council's
case this is always administratively difficult where overseas libraries
or individuals are being supplied, and sometimes against local
regulations

(2)   removal of the copying limit of one article in any one periodical
part; since in the Council's experience issues cannot be obtained
from the publisher, and there seems little distinction between
supplying several articles from several issues and the same number
from one. An alternative to removing these Regulations would be
to lift them in the case of overseas transactions.

Council for Educational Technology

509 Turning to the CET we find that it is substantially concerned with
non-book materials. Its evidence on these matters is discussed later
(751) and we deal here only with reproduction of printed matter.
Among the general points made are the following:

(1)   teachers need less restricted access to copyright material

(2)   reproductions by a teacher permitted under Section 41 of the Act
'in the course of instruction' should be similarly allowed if made
previously, or for the teacher in a resource centre, or by a pupil

(3)   educational exceptions are usually interpreted as applying in a
school — other places of instruction should be covered

(4)   copying by duplicating means is not permitted, but is essential and
should be allowed, whether by the teacher in class or elsewhere for
educational use

(5)   procedures for getting permission to copy are cumbersome and
time consuming, and material is either copied illegally or withheld
from the student.

510 CET is also concerned about the protection of rights owners and makes
these further points:

(6)   excessive copying could jeopardise publications, such as periodicals
by making them unprofitable

(7) there are few things a copyright owner can do to prevent infringements or enforce penalties; a single body representing all sectors of education to negotiate agreements is lacking, but CET is negotiating with the Publishers Association on multiple copying of print.

511 After debating these matters, the CET presents its recommendations, and suggests the following solutions (print materials being treated here in conjunction with non-book materials):

(8) the fair dealing concept should be extended to educational use, and definitions of how much is fair should be established
(9) copying within agreed limits should be permitted without the need to apply for permissions, either within the fair dealing exemptions or within the scope of agreements for remuneration to the rights owners
(10) a statutory body to decide cases of dispute is needed
(11) a body involving rights owners and educational users should also be set up
(12) the CET is willing to create the basis of such a negotiating body.

Inner London Education Authority

512 The ILEA put a more radical view in the interests of education (ref. 53). Its submission made the following points that apply to printed material:

(1) the interests of teachers, publisher and authors cannot practicably all be satisfied
(2) three solutions to the problem are possible: direct copyright control and payment, blanket agreements and indirect subsidies
(3) direct copyright control and payment imposes an impossible burden on the teacher; monitoring use by teachers is undesirable and impractical
(4) blanket agreements require crude methods of assessing what copying is being done; while publishers may be satisfied, it is difficult to see how proportional payments could be made to authors
(5) indirect subsidy is the only realistic means of benefiting authors; they should receive tax relief on income as authors
(6) any new law should be clear to all to have to work with it
(7) any new law must be enforceable
(8) public right of access to intellectual property should be regarded as at least as important as protection of commercial interest
(9) any new law should recognise changes in educational methods
(10) no solutions should impose considerable administrative burdens on teachers
(11) all educational copying should be fair dealing
(12) all activities in school, college, etc. should be regarded as educational
(13) internally produced and used teaching materials should be allowed as educational
(14) teacher in-service training, wherever held, should be recognised as educational
(15) 'test editions' should be permitted to be compiled by recognised associations
(16) tax relief for authors should be discussed by interested bodies
(17) a statutory body should consider disputes, recognise educational associations, consider cases where copyright material is being unfairly withheld against the public interest.

British Copyright Council

513 We turn now to the evidence of three bodies primarily concerned to protect copyright owners' interests. The British Copyright Council (ref. 59) made the following points:

(1) evidence that photocopying impedes implementing authors' rights is available to the Committee

(2) a study of the extent of photocopying in schools is recently completed, and when analysed will be presented to the Committee (423-4, ref. 71)

(3) blanket licensing for copying should be introduced with the dual aim of not interfering with the use of modern technology and securing a fair share of benefits to authors

(4) blanket licenses should be offered to those who wish to photocopy works under the protection of the body operating the licence.

(5) comparison is made ·with the basis on which the performing and broadcasting rights in music are administered

(6) although educational use is normally highlighted in studies of photocopying, blanket licensing should apply to all categories of user, whether in offices, post offices or railway stations.

British Printing Industries Federation

514 The BPIF notes (ref. 59) the increase in photocopying in railway stations, stores and libraries, and warns of the danger of reducing the print orders for certain types of publication to a level where the unit cost makes publication uneconomic.

Publishers Association

515 In the lengthy submission of the Publishers Association (summarised in ref. 58) the following are selected points:

(1) it continues to endorse the general licence in *Photocopying and the law*, but does not suggest its incorporation in an Act, since it could be in danger of misunderstanding as the absolute limits of permitted fair dealing copying

(2) schools copying could be covered by a blanket licence, terms to be arranged in the light of further evidence on the pattern of copying (as from the current PA/CET investigation in 70 schools, 423-4, ref. 71)

(3) collecting societies should be authorised by the Secretary of State

(4) terms of a licence should be freely negotiated, but a tribunal should be available to adjudicate in disputes

(5) if the 'general licence' were to be part of a new act, copying within its limits should not be subject to a fee

(6) blanket licensing could be extended to universities, industry and possibly further, but such arrangements should be voluntary, not statutory

(7) arrangements for copying from periodicals are satisfactory in the present Act and Regulations, though it feels some ambiguity is present in the wording, allowing the incorrect interpretation that copying of more than one article in a given issue for one person is permitted

(8) legal cases in America (Williams and Wilkins), France (Centre National de Recherche Scientifique) and Australia (University of New South Wales) show that concern over untrammelled copying

is widespread, that the restraints on copying imposed by the Act are necessary and should be clarified

(9) it doubts the legality of the BLLD's practice in its photocopy service of appointing librarians in no way connected with the BLLD as persons appointed by the librarian to receive the declarations and undertakings required by the Regulations

(10) legal deposit requirements should be modified so that only two repositories of British publications should be required, in the British Library in London, and another geographically separate; the first to be for reference, the second for loan

(11) books published in imported editions of 500 or less should be exempt from deposit, or purchased, as should be any additional copies required by other libraries

(12) the copies now sent to Trinity College Dublin are in particular resented as the library is in a country outside the Commonwealth (and not then in the EEC) and the books deposited are stifling the proper development of its Library.

Association of Learned and Professional Society Publishers

516 The Association offered some detailed comments, mostly related to photocopying. These points were made:

(1) reductions in library budgets coupled with rising journal production costs are already producing a vicious circle which can only be made worse by too easy copying facilities, leading to cessation of publication

(2) present techniques of photocopying encourage infringements of the law

(3) any person or organisation that makes photocopies could well be asked to make a payment

(4) fair dealing and the privileges of libraries should be defined in closer terms, especially in the matter of charging the full cost of copies and defining what is a reasonable proportion

(5) photocopiers should be compulsorily registered, and a collecting society established

(6) licensing arrangements should be easier to introduce once copiers are registered

(7) educational users should be treated as other users

(8) crown copyright should be modified to facilitate transfer of rights from authors to journal publishers

(9) mailing and other lists are of value and should be given copyright protection

(10) penalties, which are now no deterrent, should be increased

(11) term of copyright in revisions after an author's death should be reconsidered

(12) possible developments in computer handling should not be overlooked.

517 The ALPSP then proposed two schemes for introducing payment for photocopying. The first involves a general licence, in which the figure of 30% of a journal subscription price is suggested as a reasonable fee for permission to make up to 10 copies of an article at a time. The second scheme sets out the necessary arrangements for photocopier owners to pay directly for copies produced. This involves code numbers for journals, collecting societies, and pads of official forms. The ALPSP consider possible but do not recommend a system of officially issued stamps which have to be purchased and affixed to photocopies.

The Whitford Committee's Report on Reprography

518 Chapter 4 of the Report is titled 'Reprography'. It is broadly divided into a general introduction, a consideration of the points made in evidence, the Committee's conclusions, and a summary of recommendations. There are 88 paragraphs, and it will be impracticable to repeat all the points made: those on the Gregory Report have been discussed, others are dealt with later in chapter 8 on the international situation, and much of the evidence has already been reported. I shall try instead to give the general flavour of the Committee's thinking and any new topics or lines of thought introduced.

519 The Committee begin by noting the increase in costs of photocopying compared with those of printing, and that copying is clearly here to stay. They remark that microform and computerised rearrangements of texts all result in visually perceptible copy and are all treated as 'reprographic reproduction' or 'reprography'.

520 The Committee then deal with the Gregory Committee's recommendations and their embodiment in the 1956 Act. *Photocopying and the law* is also mentioned. Under the international situation section, the Berne and Universal conventions are mentioned briefly and the work of the International Working Group, after which a description of the position in several countries is given. In conclusion the Committee say that although blanket licences which have been introduced in other countries are not all working smoothly, they infer from this that details need careful consideration, not that such schemes are unworkable.

521 Not much of the evidence the Committee mention receiving is attributed to its source, and most of what is, comes from the organisations already mentioned in this chapter. But it must be remembered that a very wide variety of individuals and organisations, about 70 in all, did submit evidence on matters of reprography. Some of the points with which submissions from librarians were concerned were the need for simplification, the doubtful interpretation of Regulations, the dubious value of declarations, the irksomeness of administration, including difficulties over charging, and the poor return to publishers and authors which copyright fees would yield. There was also, librarians said, a need for greater relaxation of the rules where special considerations apply, such as copying for conservation, or to replace damaged copies; for security; with out-of-print works and manuscripts in public care; for space saving; and with periodicals, where the limitation to one article is unduly restrictive.

522 Organisations in the business of reprocessing information, labelled documentation centres by the Committee, were thought to be ideally suited to blanket licensing arrangements. The Committee went on to educational users, noting the extreme view of the ILEA (512), the the licensing plans of the CET, and the changes in educational methods that had led to the call for more copying. The case for individual users, at present prevented from taking advantage of the libraries' provisions was also represented to the Committee, as were the needs of the legal profession.

523   Publishers claimed that copying was already endangering periodicals and even educational books. The Ordnance Survey licence was mentioned and the Publishers Association/CET proposals. Authors were in general prepared to agree with their publishers on this issue. Several organisations mentioned the need for an arbitration body for disputes over licensing.

524   Costs of photocopying were mentioned at some length, the Committee citing a few conflicting pieces of evidence, and shrewdly concluding that in many cases copying is done not for economy, but as the easiest solution to a pressing problem. The Committee frowned on mechanical methods of preventing print from being copied (see ref. 44) as unrealistic.

Conclusions

525   The conclusions the Committee came to were as follows:

(1) educational users should be expected to pay for their copying of copyright material, and not regarded as a special case

(2) modern copying methods have made the law unworkable; as a result publications can be in danger; and a way must be found to reverse the trend

(3) most people would welcome a scheme that was simple and allowed them to copy for a modest sum

(4) suppression of copying is not the right answer to the problem; instead a form of blanket licensing should be introduced

(5) blanket licensing is defined as the copyright owners foregoing their individual rights to take action, in favour of a collecting agency which gives permissions to users to copy from any works for which the collector acts as agent, the collector then distributing the fees he collects among the owners

(6) viable schemes should in the course of time be established to cover most published works

(7) only the existence of the Libraries Regulations prevents blanket licensing from being introduced straightaway; these exceptions should be withdrawn when schemes are brought in

(8) fair dealing should not cover facsimile copying even by students: only that made by hand or typewriter

(9) details of a blanket licensing scheme should not be written into a new act

(10) to encourage schemes to be produced, reprographic copying should be freely allowed if after a stated interval, copyright owners have not introduced schemes

(11) copying by libraries, education, government, industry, the professions and copying agencies should all come under blanket licence arrangements

(12)   the number of collecting societies must be kept at a minimum, and
       they should be recognised by the Minister
(13)   a copyright tribunal should settle disputes between collecting
       societies and users
(14)   flexibility should be allowed to permit different rates for different
       users and for different classes of materials
(15)   administration should be simple so as not to absorb too much of the
       income: 10-15% seems a reasonable proportion
(16)   ministerial recognition of collecting societies would ensure proper
       conduct and fair arrangements between users and owners of copyright
(17)   for single copy photocopying to be subject to a blanket licence will
       be unpopular, but in fairness to the authors or publishers, libraries
       and others should recognise that a contribution is reasonable;
       especially in cases where copying is rate- or tax-supported
(18)   licences for users who copy a large amount of non-copyright materials
       would take this factor into account
(19)   special licences should be brought in for coin-operated machines
(20)   new legislation should make it clear that microcopies are facsimile
       copies and affected in the same way as other copies
(21)   upper limits should be set within which blanket licences should
       operate: copying which is re-publishing, for example, would not be
       allowable under the Berne Convention
(22)   unpublished work in libraries should be reprographically copiable
       under blanket licence arrangements

The foregoing considered views of the Committee are summarised into
seven separate recommendations at the end of the Chapter.

Reactions to the Whitford Committee's Report

The Library Association

526   The Library Association prepared an 'interim statement' for submission to the Department of Trade by the end of 1977, on the
Whitford Report, and this dealt principally with the Committee's
proposals on reprography. After further consideration, the interim
statement was confirmed. It makes these points:

(1)   insufficient evidence has been adduced to support the proposals for
      a blanket licensing scheme
(2)   insufficient note was taken by the Whitford Committee of the
      legitimate interest of users and libraries in having ready access to
      publicly available information; such access by making copies should
      be such as not to prejudice viable publications
(3)   the 'vicious circle' argument that copying reduces circulations which
      increases prices which again reduces circulations until publication
      ceases, is not accepted as proven in the case of single copy copying;
      but the case for multiple copying to be chargeable, perhaps by a
      blanket licensing scheme, is accepted
(4)   single extract copying from books cannot justify the conclusions
      drawn by the Committee from their consideration of journal copying;
      journal copying itself is mostly from non-profit making authors
(5)   fees for copying by libraries would have to be found from journals
      funds, thus tightening the vicious circle feared by the Committee,
      especially as most revenue would go to journals least at risk

(6) the identification of groups of copyright owners for a blanket licensing scheme would be difficult, and an administrative weakness of such a scheme

(7) that authors or publishers have suffered loss through library copying has not been proved, and it would be wrong to base legislation on facts that are in dispute; further study is needed

(8) the Aslib study on periodical renewals and cancellations should produce evidence of value, but further information about library copying and its effects should have been sought by the Committee

(9) the proposal to withdraw fair dealing provisions and the library exceptions is seen as premature; the best way of bringing copying under control is to strengthen the present provisions.

527 The L.A.'s statement concludes by welcoming the limitation of the term of copying protection to the life of the author plus fifty years; and the suggestion that national archives of audio visual materials should be established. It considers too that the financial burden of legal deposit requirements could be eased by some financial concession. The L.A. then proposed a piece of research, to be commissioned by the B.L.'s R. & D. Department, into the extent of library copying.

Standing Conference of National and University Libraries

528 SCONUL began its comments by roundly declaring it could not support the Committee's proposals on reprography. In detail it makes the following points:

(1) the Committee attaches insufficient importance to the communication of information and ideas

(2) the 'vicious circle' argument on journal copying and publication is not proven; legislation based on the assumption without further evidence would be improper

(3) any additional revenue provided by a charge on reprography would be insufficient to break the 'vicious circle'; in fact the smaller circulation journals now at risk could be damaged further by library cancellations caused by the need to raise fees for reprography

(4) lack of detail about blanket licensing prompts queries on several points of its operation; extent of costs for libraries, direct or indirect; amount of record-keeping required; effect on inter-library loans, especially from BLLD; how fair a distribution of receipts there would be; and that to cover costs the fees would have to be substantial

(5) points made in the evidence are repeated: that fair dealing should be retained, that individuals should remain responsible for their copying actions; SCONUL is particularly opposed to making installers of coin-operated machines responsible for infringements of copyright made by others on them

(6) since most library copying is of single copies of articles for which authors receive no payment, blanket licensing seems inappropriate, and can hardly deal effectively with cases where payment is appropriate — large extracts and multiple copies

(7) tax allowances and grants would be more suitable for the salvation of endangered publications

(8) the danger of inadequate charges by libraries is overstated; harmonisation on an international level, though mentioned by the Committee, would not be achieved by their recommendations, both in the

matter of inter-library charges and the recognition of scholarship's interests

529 SCONUL also refers to the doubts aroused by the Committee's recommendation on the rights of users of unpublished papers; it is opposed to the recommendations on audio visual materials (762), and mentions the difficulties raised by computerised bibliographic records and abstracts.

530 These comments were sent to the Department of Trade in November 1977: a year later SCONUL followed up with a letter urging the Department not to implement measures without full consultation, drawing attention to the unsatisfactory progress of the United States Copyright Clearance Center and the action being taken by publishers to compensate for their disappointment over the level of financial return on payments for copying outside the exceptions permitted by the Guidelines laid down after the new Copyright Law was enacted.

Council for Educational Technology

531 The CET submitted ten pages of comments on the Report. As before it had pertinent things to say on audio visual materials and these will be considered later (765-6). Its position on reprography and other general matters can be summarised under the following points:

(1) reprography should continue to be a restricted act and blanket licensing should be introduced
(2) one scheme rather than several should be sufficient for all copyright owners for these reasons:
   (a) costs would be less
   (b) special needs (e.g. of map or music publishers) could otherwise fragment the principle
   (c) users' convenience would be served by having to approach only one body
   (d) permission to copy or perform could be addressed to one licensing body
(3) tribunal precdures should be kept simple
(4) there should not be a requirement for special licences for coin-operated machines: one licence for an educational institution should cover all modes of copying
(5) the abolition of fair dealing provisions is regretted, but seen as reasonable.

532 Further remarks concern the use of computer programmes, which CET agrees should be controlled, and ownership of copyright in works commissioned or made by employees, where CET sees difficulties of interpreting the phrase: exploitation 'within the contemplation of the parties'. The CET also points out that the Committee have not specifically dealt with photographs taken by employees, in which case it thinks copyright should be as with other employees' works. It also welcomes the general exception that is proposed under which non-reprographic fair dealing should be permitted for all purposes that do not conflict with normal exploitation, but considers it undesirable to specify that research should be private. The CET concludes its remarks by regretting that the Committee could not see fit to recognise the special needs of education, and that under the Committee's proposals some educational institutions will be worse off than under the 1956 Act.

University of London Library Resources Co-ordinating Committee

533 The University produced a lengthy response to the Report, of which the greater part was to do with photocopying. The sections dealing with audio visual materials and computers will be considered in a later chapter (763, 780). Points made on reprography include the following:

(1) any restriction on copying hinders learning and scholarship

(2) the Committee's view that installers of self-service copiers should be held responsible for infringing copies made on them is challenged: the individual requiring the copy should be responsible

(3) if the person requiring is made formally repsonsible, the need for declarations will be removed

(4) multiple copying is usually of only a few pages; such copies should be allowed since they replace single copies legally made separately for a multiple audience; such multiple copying would be reduced by implementing the Royal Society 1948 recommendations for more separates to be distributed

(5) copying by libraries should not jeopardise periodicals' survival; there is little evidence for it, and it is libraries that purchase many copies. Authors are less dependent on income than upon prestige from publication

(6) copying for preservation is also necessary to libraries, both in supplying copies instead of loans and in microfilming for storage

(7) title pages and contents lists, and extracts from publishers and booksellers catalogues need to be copied by libraries in current awareness and selection processes

(8) damaged or missing pages need to be copied from other copies to maintain integrity of works

(9) some of these requirements are recognised by the Whitford Committee but no recommendations are made for them

(10) administrative difficulties in working a blanket licence scheme may have been underestimated by the Committee, especially that of distributing income: the only just method would be to record each copying transaction in every library

(11) the levels of charging and ways of assessing fees are not gone into; relevance of royalty payments for music performance is doubted

(12) whatever happens in blanket licensing the cost of education would rise

(13) fair dealing provisions should be retained and clarified; the restriction to one article in any one periodical part should be relaxed

(14) copyright in laws, judgements and parliamentary proceedings should be relaxed for all copying purposes short of republication; unreported decisions of the Court of Appeal should be available through other channels than the Association of Official Shorthandwriters

(15) the Committee's recommendation to end perpetual copyright in unpublished works could inhibit deposits of important collections of papers; safeguards need to be built, and any legislation to protect depositors' interests

(16) if royalties are introduced for library copying, it should be illegal

for publishers to charge differentially higher prices for services to libraries.

534 The University of London also supports the proposal for a seventh deposit library (John Rylands University Library of Manchester), considering deposit copies no great burden and comparing them with review copies (frequently unproductive); copies deposited can be accounted payment by publishers for the automatic conferral of copyright and its maintenance (e.g. through international conferences). Audio visual archives are also supported.

Royal Society

535 The Society's comments on the Report, though considerably briefer are especially wide ranging. Apart from remarks on computers, considered later, the Society makes the following points:

(1) the fair copying declaration principle of access to scientific knowledge is reiterated
(2) the proposal to restrict fair dealing to hand and typewriter copying could damage scientifice research
(3) administrative problems and costs of a blanket licensing scheme have not been adequately accounted for; and the proposal seems not to have taken into account overseas experience in this area
(4) the case of maps needs clarifying, as much information on current Ordnance Survey maps is unchanged from earlier, out of copyright editions, thereby suggesting a different interpretation of what constitutes a substantial part of a map that is to be copied
(5) the Committee's recommendation for photographs, that the copyright should be held by the person responsible for composition, is very well for artistic photographs, but inadequate for scientific, e.g. aerial photography. It should also be made clear that data in photographs can be extracted without infringement.

536 Reactions from organisations representing copyright owners, such as the Publishers Association and the Society of Authors, in general welcomed the Report for its recognition of their copyright problems, its firm proposals to introduce payment rewards for use, and no less its very readable style (see refs. 52, 57, 66).

537 One cautionary note was struck in a letter to the Times Literary Supplement in June 1977 by Peter du Sautoy of Faber and Faber on the subject of copyright in unpublished documents deposited in institutions. The Committee were wrong in saying that the recipient of private letters can make them publicly available, unless they meant to sell them or make them available in a library or similar institution. Publishing them was not now permitted. Mr. du Sautoy was also concerned at the Committee's suggestion that an author who did not want something he had written to become public property should retain it and destroy it before he died. Clearly this would be impossible with most letters, and it was desirable that authors and their heirs should be reassured on the point that the Whitford Committee did not intend they should lose copyright protection in unpublished works that passed out of their physical possession.

E. H. Ratcliffe : Notes on copyright

538 In July 1979 a further exposition of the law appeared (ref. 12a) by Eric H. Ratcliffe, a technical editor in industry, which combined an account of the law as it applied to technical writers and information workers, with some comments on the Whitford Report and suggestions for the future shape of legislation. Under the heading 'Copyright in unpublished literary works', Ratcliffe gives a warning about the need for companies to keep control of internally produced work, especially in the case of employees who leave the company. Extempore presentations are also relevant here as the copyright is not established until they are written down. He notes that periodical publishers actually have only a typographical copyright in articles submitted unless an assignment is made, though of course they do have an implied licence to publish in that format. There is a lengthy discussion of reprographic reproduction by libraries and other institutions which gives a brief account of what is currently permitted (see 539 for comments on this), and the discussions of the Whitford Committee. Of computers, Ratcliffe finds Whitford's conclusions 'over-simplified', and doubts whether copyright will give programs more protection than normal trade secrecy. There is a section headed 'Miscellaneous', which embraces brief notes on commissioned works; papers sent to periodicals, which physically become the property of the recipient without an obligation to publish, though authors will retain some rights against changes made to them unless copyright is assigned in writing to the publisher; on translations; on abstracts; on fair dealing, though without mentioning who can take advantage of it; on 'substantial part'; and on cautions found in published materials against copying. The final paragraph concerns Crown copyright, and a useful section on Ordnance Survey maps and publications. In this last connection Ratcliffe refers to O.S. Leaflet 23, but readers are reminded of a special notice for librarians, published in my own Handbook (ref. 16, Vol. 2 p.881-2).

539 In setting out what the law permits, Mr. Ratcliffe makes in my opinion a few errors:

    (1)   He thinks most special libraries are able to use the Libraries Regulations, since they are established for 'study in a field approved by a schedule in the Regulations.' As I point out earlier (106, 237), this is not the usual interpretation.

    (2)   He has misread the Regulations to read that a librarian may supply copies to any library provided it (the receiving library) is available freely to the public. However, the wording of the Regulations is quite clear 'no copy shall be supplied to the librarian of any library that is established or conducted for profit.'

    (3)   He states that libraries may supply copies of complete periodicals to

each other. This is negated, though not forcibly, by the Regulations wording that only 'an article in a periodical publication' may be supplied without permission being sought.

(4)   When dealing with parts of non-periodical items for library users, he fails to include the important proviso that permission must be sought before copies may be made of a substantial, or reasonable part.

A.L.C.S. and Wolfenden Group

540   A few developments since Whitford are worth mentioning. There have been the first moves on the part of the copyright owners to prepare for legislation involving royalty payments for photocopying. This has taken two forms, first the establishment of the Authors' Lending and Copyright Society, which proposes to act as a collecting agency by registering authors at a nominal sum and collecting payments, initially from the government in respect of public lending right entitlements, but later also for copying royalties when legislation is brought in, or earlier if voluntary agreements are reached with copyright user groups. The second move complements this, and is the formation in mid-1977 of the Wolfenden Group, representing many types of copyright owner, both literary and musical. The Group is trying to set up voluntary licensing agreements whereby copyright users can copy materials within defined limits without needing to seek permission but on payment of fees. Since much single copy copying is permitted at present under the 1956 Act, the Committee is concentrating on multiple copying, and the first negotiations have been between copyright owners and Scottish schools, but at the time of writing agreement had not been finalised.

Music Publishers Association 'Copying Music'

541   In September 1979, the Music Publishers Association issued a pamphlet *Copying music*, subtitled 'a code of fair practice agreed between composers, publishers and users.' This carries the blessing of 25 organisations, including the International Association of Music Libraries (U.K. Branch). It offers copying without permission within strictly defined limits of works copyrighted by a list of 89 organisations, which includes the major music publishers. The circumstances in which copies may be made are ten in number, and cover (1) emergencies, for example when music for a performance has been lost or damaged (in these cases the copy may not be retained by the user); (2) performance difficulies, e.g. to obviate awkward page turns — but less than a performable unit is the limit here; (3) study and research, under which short excerpts (of less than performable units) may be copied; (4) extra parts for orchestra or band parts, or classroom sets (up to a quarter set, provided one full set has been bought or hired); (5) up to five string parts from orchestral sets, to retain bowing and fingering marks; (6) out of print works, provided the copier gives three weeks notice to the publisher and obtains his permission; (7) in cases of non-supply or ordered music, again after giving due notice to the publishers; (8) extracts from complete editions, again after contacting the publisher; (9) chorus material in vocal scores, subject to limitation of 10 per cent of the total vocal score, (and non-availability of separate chorus parts); (10) other permissions must be negotiated.

542   This list is necessarily summarised, and for full details the pamphlet, which is free, should be consulted. Most of the circumstances will not be encountered by the librarian, but one should note that there are no further restrictions on who may make copies. 'The benefit of this code is open to any music user . . . Permission shall apply equally to organisations as to individuals, and to others acting on behalf of the intending user.' There is also a list of seven prohibitions. Copies may not be made: to evade purchase or hire; of approval or inspection copies; of whole works or complete movements (except under permissions 4, 5, 8 & 9); of hired works (except under 4 & 5); to make anthologies; of 'consumables' such as workbooks; and copies made may not be sold or hired. The library interest is principally catered for under permission 3, for study and research. Note that this need not be for private study, but since only excerpts or less than performable units may be made under this permission, it probably allows little more than is copiable as 'not a substantial part'. See 498-9 for further discussion of library copying of music.

543   And there, at the time of writing, the matter rests. Three years after publication of the Whitford Report no government action has been taken. (For international developments see 833-850). The government that received all the comments on Whitford by the end of 1977 was of a different political persuasion from the one that now has to consider action. It may be that the ground covered by the Report was too large, and indeed too diverse, to be incorporated in one piece of legislation, and we may have to wait longer (Ratcliffe's estimate is between 1979-86) before the Committee's recommendations are dealt with. However, a green (consultative) paper has been promised by the Department of Trade before the end of 1980.

6
The Periodicals Debate: Does Copying Harm Sales?

601   Since the Royal Society's Fair Copying Declaration of 1950, by which a group of periodical publishers, including several in the business for profit, agreed to allow libraries to make single copies of articles without charge, there has been a gradually increasing reluctance among publishers in general to agree that library photocopying does no harm to their circulations. But in 1950 and until the early 1960's library copying was a laborious business, usually by contact photography, not readily paraded as an on-demand service, and not cheap in materials or labour, though the equipment was not particularly costly. Came the Xerox machine, first in the shape of the large Copyflo, with its microfilm intermediate stage and then the handier 914, and copying was suddenly far easier.

Williams & Wilkins v. National Library of Medicine

602   However, it was not until 1968 that murmurs began to be heard from publishers that copying was being too freely indulged in. In the United States, the firm of Williams and Wilkins Inc., publishers of 37 medical journals, claimed that excessive photocopying had driven two of their journals out of publication, and that they were losing subscriptions on others. The chief culprit they saw as the National Library of Medicine, which was offering a free photocopy service, and so a lawsuit was begun in which Williams and Wilkins sued the United States Government for infringement of their copyright through the National Institutes of Health and the National Library of Medicine.

603   Under the American law, which was at that time the Copyright Law of 1909, no express permissions for copying by libraries — such as the British 1956 Act afford — were available as a defence. The principal defence was one of 'fair use' which in American law was as difficult to elucidate as fair dealing in British law, but in general had the same purpose: to permit non-competitive copying. There was also a 'gentlemen's agreement' between publishers and libraries that dated back to 1937 by which copying could be done by libraries provided the library warned the recipient of the copy about infringing use; that the library made no profit on the copy; and the amount copied was not substantial.

604 It took the U.S. Court of Claims until 1972 to come to a decision, when Commissioner Davis found for the plaintiffs that their copyright had been infringed. Various arguments were put up by the defendants, some of them surprising in their ineptness, and looking for loopholes in the law rather than constructing a valid fair use defence. The Commissioner gave his opinion that 'Whatever may be the bounds of 'fair use' as defined and applied by the courts, defendant is clearly outside those bounds'. The U.S. law he said did not require the plaintiff to prove actual damages (i.e. loss of subscriptions) to establish his case, but this was done by the fact that the copies made were intended as substitutes for the original and thereby diminished the plaintiff's market. In addition, Commissioner Davis referred to evidence that had been brought that at least two customers had cancelled their subscriptions because of the availability of photocopies. Before the Court came to this decision there had been several briefs filed by outside parties as 'amici curiae' (friends of the court) representing points of view both of proprietors and users of journals and other publications. These were admitted because it was recognised that the Williams and Wilkins case was a 'ground-breaking' one.

Verdicts

605 The U.S. Government, however, appealed against this decision in the Court of Claims, and was successful. In 1973 they held the government free of liability, but the decision was reached by a majority vote, and one of the dissenting judges gave a lengthy opinion. This encouraged Williams and Wilkins to take the case to the Supreme Court, but disappointingly for both sides the Supreme Court was deadlocked in a 4-4 verdict, which effectively left the Government in possession, though without establishing the decision as a precedent for lower courts. In delivering the Court of Claims verdict the speaker, another Judge Davis, made the point that fair use could in certain circumstances embrace the making of a complete copy, and directed attention to the need for 'accommodating the interests of science with those of the publishers and authors'. The appeal court's decision was that there was no evidence of loss of income to the publisher: that the four journals in question had all increased their subscriptions, that the firm's profits had increased, and that this increase was above the rate of increase of the gross national product. 'The record' they said, 'is also barren of solid evidence that photocopying has caused economic harm to any other publisher of medical journals'. The plaintiff's claim that it had lost income from licensing schemes that it had offered to the N.L.M. for the right to copy was irrelevant, since the judgement had first to be made on whether use was unfair before plaintiff had the right to impose such a scheme.

606 The dissenting Chief Judge Cowen, on the other hand, said the plaintiffs' income 'does not reflect the effect of defendant's photocopying of
plaintiff's journals, and particularly the effect it will have on the
prospects for continued success in the future'. He went on to say that
proof of actual damages is not required, but potential damage had
been held to be sufficient reason to discount the fair use defence. In
this particular case Cowen held that 'the photocopying . . . has had a
tendency to diminish plaintiff's markets in the past'.

607 One of the reasons this case dragged on for six years was the failure
of the plaintiff to prove damages, which allowed all kinds of arguments
to be adduced on both sides in the effort to reach a settlement. As
Cowen said: 'The court recognises that the solution which it has
undertaken to provide in this case is pre-eminently a problem for
Congress which should decide how much photocopying should be
allowed, what payments should be made to copyright owners, and
related quesions. Nowhere else in its opinion is the court on more solid
ground than when it declares that the "choices involve social and
policy factors which are far better sifted by a legislature" '.

British Library Lending Division

608 The U.S. Congress did in fact pass a new Copyright Law towards the
end of 1976, and made detailed provision for library photocopying in
it, which will be examined later. In the meantime, with the unsatisfactory split verdict from the U.S. Supreme Court, attention focussed
again in this country on the British Library Lending Division (BLLD),
whose photocopy service was similar to that of the NLM though on
a much larger scale, covering as it did all subjects and all types of
periodical above the exclusively popular. In late 1974 the Whitford
Committee had been set up, giving publishers and librarians a hope,
distant but distinct, of new legislation, and the clear possibility that
BLLD's practice of providing photocopied articles would at least be
called in question.

Garfield and Sophar vs Urquhart

609 Back in 1970, Messrs. Garfield and Sophar had written (ref. 9) to
challenge the assumption that the BLLD's former self the National
Lending Library for Science and Technology was acting legally in its
provision of copies: in many instances, they felt, 'the publisher or
author suffers financial loss'. Dr. D. J. Urquhart, the NLLST's
Director had replied that their 'fair dealing' protection had not been
removed by any precise definition of the term, and that the loss to
authors or publishers was less of a forceful argument since (a) authors
of journal articles copied by NLLST rarely received any reward,
(b) that authors themselves relied on libraries such as NLLST to help
them, and (c) that publishers were frequently out of stock of back

issues. 'It is thus unrealistic' he concluded, 'to imagine that publishers suffer any significant losses due to library copying of such items.'

Line and Wood vs van Tongeren

610 By 1975, Maurice Line, Urquhart's successor at BLLD, was able to report the results of extensive studies conducted at BLLD to discover the extent of photocopying in the library, and its distribution among the journals in their stock. In an article written with D. N. Wood, also of BLLD (ref. 30), he reports the great growth in volume of photocopied items, from 13,307 in 1963 to 893,801 in 1974. One factor in the increase was the encouragement given by BLLD to photocopies as opposed to loans, for the reason that this reduced postal costs and improved the service, since a copied journal is still available for a further request, which would be delayed if it was on loan. Another factor was the amalgamation of NLLST with NCL in 1973 to broaden the subject coverage of the new BLLD.

611 Line and Wood then offer what evidence they can find on journal publishing. A sample of journals showed an overall increase of about 10% in circulation; British journals, in a separate sample, had only 5% increase. The rates of increase and of mortality of journals are constant over the period. However the costs of journals had increased rapidly, and Line and Wood give a table to show that real value (allowing for retail price index and pages published) decreased by 17% from 1960-73, with society journals losing 28% against 7% from commercial journals.

612 This information suggests that over the period 1965-71 libraries would have needed to increase their periodical spending by 17%, and though figures for industrial libraries were not available, university libraries were found to have had an overall increase in expenditure of 17%–18%. Further figures, again from university libraries, show that from 1950/51 to 1971/72 periodical expenditure increased in proportion to book expenditure and in proportion to total expenditure, and there was a slight increase also in the percentage of total university expenditure devoted to libraries. The overall position however, was not improving, and libraries were now (1974-75) having to cancel some subscriptions, but 'could hardly be spending more than they do on journals, whether or not photocopies were being provided from the BLLD or anywhere else. It is possible, indeed probable that they would plead a stronger case for larger funds if photocopies could not be supplied, but it is very doubtful indeed whether their institutions could provide them'.

613 Line and Wood then refer to a Library Association small survey of various libraries, which found that journal cancellations had nearly doubled in a year. Reasons for cancellation, however, rarely included availability from other libraries. Likeliest candidates for cancellation were 'fringe interest' titles and those of which several copies were formerly taken. Line and Wood also believe that the extra large increase in photocopying at BLLD could be accounted for principally by extra demand created by the existence of a fast and efficient service and was not an alternative to local purchase.

614 Looking further into the photocopy details they note that of all requests for serials, 40% were met by loans, and of the remaining 60%, half (30%) were of items more than three years old and therefore unlikely to be in stock at publishers. Analysis of the large sample survey that produced these figures also showed a considerable concentration of requests on relatively few titles. Out of 14,967 titles in the survey, 50% of requests were from only 1,400 and not much more than half (8,300) of the titles were responsible for 90% of requests. This leads Line and Wood to the conclusion that 'many of those [journals] for which recent circulation figures could be found have large circulations which would hardly be threatened even by a much larger quantity of copying than that carried out by BLLD'. A table given by Line and Wood shows 78 journal titles of which over 300 photocopies are estimated to be made by BLLD from the last 3 years' issues. Only the first two rise above 1,000 photocopies, and another 19 above 500. These titles have circulations (where known) ranging from 4,500 to 500,700. They go on to suggest that 'any library expecting more than seven or eight uses a year' of the current or recent issues of a periodical would find it cheaper to buy than to borrow.

615 Another way of looking at these figures is suggested: BLLD's photocopies in a year of journals up to three years old would be about 500,000, but these copies would be taken from a population of about 4.2 million articles published in those three years. The average one in eight chance of an article being copied by BLLD rises only to just over one in three in the case of *Science*, the most frequently copied journal, and about one in two for *The Lancet*, the most frequently copied British journal.

616 Having presented all this evidence of a minimal impact on publishing economics by BLLD's copying activities, Line and Wood then consider more problematic matters. If photocopying were not offered as a service, they say, more copies of the popular journals might be bought but this would mean cutting out altogether some low use titles. They discount the effect of the BLLD's service on library budgets — there would be only a fractional increase in sales to other libraries or individuals. If publishers charged BLLD more for their journals, BLLD in turn would buy fewer or pass on the extra costs to their users. If a royalty had to be paid for photocopies and if this rate were

5p a copy, even *Science*, the most requested journal, would receive only £220 in a year, even if all articles were included.

617   Line and Wood conclude their article by saying that BLLD's expansion of the photocopying service and the problems facing journal publishers are not cause and effect, but two effects of the same cause: 'an increasingly constrained library and individual market at the same time as the volume and cost of publications have continued to increase'.

618   This article was replied to by E. van Tongeren, of Associated Scientific Publishers, Amsterdam (ref. 42). His main concern was that Line and Wood's article obscured the problems that scientific journal publishers were facing, and gave the reader 'a false sense of the stability of journal publishing'. He quoted a journal editor saying:

> 'The act of copying is not the damaging element. The use of modern technology to speed and increase the dissemination of knowledge is desirable and to be encouraged. But dissemination from an expensive information base without contributing to its support is certain to lead to erosion of something of great value: the information base itself, or in simpler terms, the scientific journal system.'

619   Without being in a posiion to prove the point, van Tongeren is convinced that BLLD's activities are influencing cancellation decisions. He finds Line and Wood's statistics unconvincing in that they take insufficient account of the large, expensive, small circulation journals that are the backbone of scientific journal publishing. He notes that BLLD is subsidising its users in each act of lending or photocopying (75p. marginal cost against 46p. charge); and draws sarcastic parallels between occasional free use of an expensive information base and other commercial services. He sees this principle as undermining the structure of primary scientific publishing. He finds Line and Wood's suggested 5p. per article as a royalty derisory, and asks why not 25p. and why not charge by the page. In conclusion he says it is 'undeniable that the present economic climate is very unfavourable' and asks why Line and Wood should think it justifiable to 'hasten the decline [of publishing ventures] by the creation of super- and networking-libraries who without thought for the future expect their raw materials to be supplied free of charge . . . Entitlement to make single copies *as a matter of right* should be removed from the existing law'.

620   Line and Wood answered this lengthy 'documention note' in the same issue, largely rebutting van Tongeren's arguments by expanding on or explaining their original article. One point may be extracted: the figure of 5p. and not as van Tongeren suggested 25p. for a notional royalty was chosen because at the higher rate libraries would borrow instead of ordering photocopies and copy themselves. The NLLST copying practice had begun because it was noticed that libraries were returning loans as soon as they were received, and it was obvious they were being copied in libraries. Finally Line and Wood remark the need for facts in discussing the effect of copying on sales, and draw attention to a (then) forthcoming study on trends in scholarly publishing.

Fry and White

621 An important American study had become available during 1975, and was known as the 'Fry and White Report', (Economics and interaction of the publisher-library relationship in the production and use of scholarly and research journals.) This was eventually published in 1976, (ref. 121, see also ref. 45). It presented evidence from surveys carried out between 1969 and 1973, and sought to discover the effects on library practice of economic pressures in relation to journal holdings. It also examined publishers' problems in this field. Chapter 6 described borrowing and lending activities. In the survey it was found that libraries could not distinguish statistically between borrowing and obtaining a photocopy of a document, and thus, some potentially useful information eluded the team.

622 The point was made that even when an item is borrowed, it is frequently copied before being returned to the lending library, so the distinction was of less significance than might have been supposed. It could therefore be assumed that in the case of short journal articles (10 pages or less) borrowing included copying, and what was found to be true of borrowing could be said of copying. Fry and White report that up to 1973 among academic libraries 40% reported an impact on subscriptions from borrowing practices. This appeared to be true particularly of large libraries, which reported reducing multiples, cancelling singles and also deciding against new subscriptions. Among public libraries about a third reported some impact, and special libraries gave insufficient data for a finding to be presented.

Nasri

623 A smaller study, and one hamstrung by the failure of its author to obtain all the data he really required was that of William Z. Nasri, who focussed his investigation on the hypothesis that scientific and technical journals and medical journals in particular were losing subscriptions because of reprography. Nasri chose to study the four journals in suit in the Williams and Wilkins case, but was unable to obtain subscription lists from the publisher, and so had to posit these journal readerships from other sources. From his survey of potential readers (his response rate was 42% for 803 questionnaires sent to individuals working in those medical fields considered likely to have an interest in the journals), Nasri found that while photocopying facilities were not a significant factor in not taking or ceasing to take a journal, likely availability was highly significant.

624 It should be emphasised that while the facts we have cited from the Fry and White study were concerned with library subscriptions, the Nasri study was of individual subscriptions. The one does not, therefore, exactly confirm the other. It should also be noted that Nasri conducted his survey in 1970-71, though it was not published until 1976: his findings, too, were set out before the result of the Williams and Wilkins case in late 1974.

King Research

625 A closer follow-up to the Fry and White report was commissioned by the National Commission on Libraries and Information Science in 1976 from King Research, Inc., specifically on 'Library photocopying in the United States'. This was required for the implementation of the new U.S. Copyright Law, signed in 1976 to come into force on 1st January 1978. More detailed attention is given to the Law's provisions later, but here we note clause (g) of Section 108, which allows libraries to make isolated photocopies except where there is reason to suppose such copying is amounting to multiple copying either for individuals or a group, and except in the case of inter-library copy supply, if it is tending to substitute for a subscription to or purchase of a work by the library receiving the copies. This last proviso led to the establishment of guidelines from the National Commission on the New Technological Uses of Copyright Works (CONTU) which will also be examined later. CONTU envisaged that copying beyond the Guidelines' provision could be licensed, and that a Copy Payments Center would need to be set up to handle transactions. King Research Inc's. study was made in this context.

626 Using a sample of photocopying in a statified sample of libraries over a six week period and weighting the sample with data from the network MINITEX for a whole year, King Research came up with these conclusions:

(1) About 114 million items were photocopied by library staff in 1976
(2) About 54 million items were of copyright materials
(3) Public (64 m.) Special (26 m.) Academic (17 m.) and Federal (7 m.) libraries made up the grand total
(4) Proportions of copyright material copied varied between type of library from 69% (special) to 37% (public)
(5) Books (14.9 m.), periodicals (48 m.) and other materials (50.8 m.) made up the 114 m. and of the books 84% and of the serials 79% were copyright, compared with 7% of the other materials
(6) 38 million serial items in copyright were copied of which most (22 m.) were for local users, and therefore permitted free of royalty under the CONTU guidelines
(7) 12 million serial items were made for intra-system loans and 4 m. for inter-library loans
(8) Requests for domestic (US published) serials amounted to 3.8 m. of which 3.1 m. were in copyright
(9) When CONTU guidelines are applied 2.4 m. of the 3.1 m. are under under six years old, and 2 m. are both under six years *and*

not used for replacement or classroom use. When the Guidelines
on number of permitted requests free of royalty is applied only
about 500,000 items are subject to royalty payment. This total goes
up to 1.9 m. if items over five years are included.

627   It may be noted that the bar of more than five copies was set because
it had been calculated that at six loans per year, it became more
economic to purchase the average periodical. This was borne out by
V. E. Palmour et al, *Cost of owning, borrowing and disposing of
periodical publications* (1977), who found that at $3 per loan cost,
the crucial point in maintaining a journal in a library, with 10 years
backfile, came between 5 and 6 issues per year for a $40 subscription.

628   In their conclusions, King Research, Inc. speculate on the effect on
subscription levels of introducing royalty payments. "We hypothesize
that, if cancellations occurred, they would have the most negative
(i.e. adverse) impact on small, specialized journals".

Whitford Report

629   King Research, Inc's. study was published in 1977 by which time the
British Whitford Report had been published. In that, as has been seen,
was a clear acceptance as a fact that library copying adversely affected
circulation levels of journals: 'unless something is done there is a
serious danger that, in some fields at least, publication will cease . . .
the increase in library and other copying means small circulations;
which means higher costs; which in its turn means more copying. In
the end publication ceases'.

630   In its response to the Whitford Report the Library Association asked
that a large-scale survey of library photocopying practices should be
made 'so that facts on this central issue are not in dispute'. Unfortunately, it was impossible to find a body skilful enough, and sufficiently
distant from the issues involved that was ready to take on the project.

Aslib's periodical subscriptions study

631   One partial piece of evidence, however, was produced when Aslib
published the results of their study of *Factors affecting the renewal of
periodical subscriptions* in 1978 (ref. 47). The survey was of 250
academic, research and industrial libraries during 1977. It was found
that in 1976 journal cancellations for the first time exceeded additions.
The rate of borrowing from other libraries was statistically unrelated
to changes in the number of subscriptions. The motives expressed by
respondents and influencing cancellations were first user advice, use
measures and price, then alternative availability (including via inter-
library lending), duplication, and subject content overlap between
journals. Interlibrary lending has also helped as being faster, cheaper
and more reliable than purchase of back issues. 15% of the respondents

said that interlibrary lending had enabled them to reduce subscriptions without damaging their service. In this study there was found to be little clear correlation between journal cancellation and borrowing either as a library policy or an inevitable consequence; changes were 'determined more by financial limitations and by user requirements than by deliberate policy or by assessments vis-à-vis journal purchase.'

632 However, it was noted that the great majority of libraries in this survey preferred photocopies to be supplied instead of loans of the original except where several articles in an issue were wanted, or the journal was borrowed as an inspection copy, or where the quality of illustration was important. The survey concludes: 'The vast majority of loans do seem to end up as photocopies'.

633 This statement is supported by a separate but associated 'loans tracking study' of requests satisfied by BLLD, made in August 1977. The sample was structured to give 75% photocopies supplied and 25% loans. Of the returns received, 23% related to loans. Of this 23%, 68% were then photocopied after receipt. This suggests that of BLLD's journal requests, 92.1% are supplied to the eventual user as photocopies. The main purpose of the loans tracking study, however, was to discover how much BLLD borrowing was 'replacement borrowing' for journals that the library had once taken. The figure discovered was 3%, but 13.3% of the loans were of journals still being received by the library.

634 The study of journal cancellations, however, is only a partial coverage of the place of the BLLD in substitution for journal subscription. As the survey points out, 'one unanswered question is what effect the 81% of loans which are for journals never taken by the borrowing library may have on the future acquisitions of the library; whether those journals might have been bought had there been no lending and borrowing of materials between libraries'.

635 This study had been sponsored through Aslib by the International Group of Scientific, Technical and Medical Publishers (known widely as STM). It is worth remarking that STM's retiring chairman in 1977 was Mr. Bart van Tongeren. STM was much concerned about what they see as 'erosion of copyright' by photocopying: their 'ultimate goal is that all copying should be subject to a fair remuneration of the copyright holders'. When the Aslib study was published, Mr. Paul Nijhoff Asser, secretary of STM, accepted the finding that there was no clearly direct link between photocopying and journal cancellation, but called attention to the 15% of libraries the report had found who said that interlibrary lending had enabled them to reduce subscriptions without damaging their services (ref. 27).

636 So there the debate rests: no proofs have been brought forward on either side of the Atlantic that single copy photocopying of journals by libraries has any direct influence on library or individual subscriptions to those journals. But the publishers, while not disputing the findings of research studies, adhere to the view that the general climate of availability of library services free or at low cost is having a seriously limiting effect on their realising their full sales potential, and that librarians in their defences are taking too short term or blinkered a view of the threats to journal publication.

7
Microforms, Audio Visual Materials and Computers

701 In this chapter I wish to bring out first a few points regarding micro-forms that could be overlooked if they are regarded simply as printed matter, then go on to discuss the more complex issues surrounding works that are audio, or visual or audio-visual, and finally consider some aspects of copyright in computer use.

Microforms

702 The Gregory Committee in its 1952 report was fully aware of the facility of microfilming, and was asked to look kindly on the practice of some libraries that made microfilmed copies of whole works either for interlending or on occasion for supplying an overseas library with a copy of a rare work of interest for its permanent retention. But the Committee saw no reasons to recommend that this practice be a right granted to libraries except where copyright owners proved impossible to locate. In their recommendation they made no distinction between methods of copying — whether microphotography or contact photo-graphy — and there is no mention of microforms in the resulting 1956 Act. Consequently, in the legal expositions of the Act, since there has been no case law on the matter either, one looks in vain for any discussion of the copyright problems of microforms.

703 Microforms can be produced in three principal ways: by direct print-ing, as in the now rare microcard or microprint (usually opaque); by photography of existing typescript, print or manuscript; and by laser or holograph production from a computerised data base (as in computer output microfilm of library catalogues). For the first and third cases, the microform is the first format of publication of that particular set of information, and copyright inheres in it as in any literary, artistic or dramatic work. But in the case of microforms that are copies of originals there are two copyrights possibly involved: that of the original which is copied, and that of the microform that results, which has its own copyright as a photograph, provided it is made legally and is not an infringing copy.

704 To deal with this last type of microform first, all the complexities of the law may come into play at its making. If the materials copied are all out of copyright the matter is relatively simple: the only copyright that subsists is in the arrangement of images or frames on the film; if there is an introduction or notes to the text added by the publisher of the microfilm they bear their own literary copyright as well as partaking of the photographic copyright. Microform photographic copyright protection lasts for fifty years after the end of the year of publication, but it is possible for literary etc, works represented on it to be still in copyright, since literary etc. copyright lasts for fifty years after the end of the year in which the author, artist, etc. died. Few published microforms, however, that are over fifty years old are yet likely to be met with in libraries. When there are more there may be some difficulties in establishing their date of publication or location of the copyright owners, for this purpose.

Substantial part

705 Bearing in mind that microform copyright is principally photographic, it will be seen that the fair dealing Section 6 and the libraries exceptions Section 7 of the 1956 Act do not apply as they concern literary, dramatic and musical works. The only protection for the would-be copier is in the fair dealing clause 9(1) and (2) and the general one of Section 49 which provides that infringement does not take place unless a 'substantial part' of a work is copied. Since there are no libraries exceptions for artistic works it could perhaps be claimed that libraries are entitled to the protection of copying under Section 9(1) for research or private study, or 9(2) for criticism or review. It is as difficult as ever to decide what a substantial part of a microform publication might be, and there are no opinions or precedents to guide one. It would seem, however, to be right to relate 'substantial' to the size of the photograph (whether on reels of film or in separate 'fiches). To take one article from a microfilmed roll of a periodical run could possibly be defended. Difficulties arise beyond this level, especially as single microform publications by their nature frequently extend over a considerable number of original pages and even of titles or volumes, and to copy what might be a small percentage from one microform publication could still be seen as a substantial proportion in terms of an individual original. These doubts apply of course only to microforms of works themselves out of copyright. The extreme case would be of a microform publisher going to great trouble to secure scarce, even unique originals of short, out-of-copyright works — say a series of broadsides — and making them available in microform. If the collection was small his sales potential could quickly be reduced by piecemeal copying.

706 It should be made clear that the copyright in microforms is infringeable by either duplicating the microform itself or by making enlargements from it. The decision on infringement would come in both instances from the amount copied. It could hardly be held that to copy a single page of illustrations from a microform of a work that was out of copyright was an infringement, since the microform's photographic copyright is in the photography, not the quality or importance of a part of the original. An exception to this might be upheld, however, in the case of the only coloured page being copied from a colour microform. These matters are difficult to resolve not because of the shortcomings of the law so much as the lack of generally accepted lay opinion — which in many law suits is frequently decisive where there is no explicit statute and no case history exists.

707   Thus far we have discussed the handling of published microforms. Before leaving them we should look at the definition of publication, and see how far it is relevant. If microforms are photographic they secure copyright at the time of publication, and this lasts for fifty years. There is of course the question of when does publication take place; if the production of sufficient copies for the reasonable requirements of the public is the criterion, microform publishers are in some difficulty. Copies are frequently made only on demand — there being little economy in production runs — and in some cases only a negative is held, no positive copies being made until orders are received, which could be years later. A commonsense definition could be: when announcement to the public of availability is made: provided at least a negative had by then been made.

708   There are fewer problems with microform originals that are not photographs or direct print: these usually have literary copyright, as for example *British Books in Print* or *Books in English,* since the arrangement of the data is copyright by the publishers. One can imagine a classical work, such as a Dickens story, being keyboarded *in toto* into a computer for purposes, say, of linguistic analysis: it would be possible to printout the whole text in the same sequence as the original, onto microform (or onto ordinary printout paper for that matter) and gain copyright protection under Section 15 for the typographic arrangement thereby created.

709   Going on from fair or otherwise use of existing microforms, it is necessary to remind readers that creating microforms is similarly a potentially infringing act. For example a library wishing to make better use of storage space may decide to microfilm back runs of journals, but if these are less than fifty years old, it is an infringement to microfilm them without the publisher's permission. It makes no difference whether the library destroys or otherwise disposes of the originals, the change of format constitutes an act of copying. Nor does it alter the case if no comparable set of microforms is available for purchase. Of course, most publishers will grant these permissions for

a modest fee, or refer the library to an agent licensed to sell micro-copies or to negotiate permissions.

710 Since a microform publication is usually a photograph it cannot be claimed by the legal deposit libraries under Section 15 of the 1911 Act. Nor have we come across any cases of these libraries claiming printed microforms or those produced by other non-photographic methods. There is thus no deposit collection of generally published microforms in this country.

Whitford Committee evidence : Microfilm Association of Great Britain

711 The setting up of the Whitford Committee was naturally the occasion for representations to be made on matters concerning copyright in microforms. The Microfilm Association of Great Britain, whose members are from the trade and users alike, made the following points in their evidence (ref. 88):

(1) Publication should be defined as the making of a microform master
(2) Micro transparencies should be explicitly covered by legislation
(3) Protection similar to that for typographic arrangement should be afforded to the microform publisher in respect of the format, arrangement of images, added front-matter, indexes, etc.
(4) Copying of the whole or a substantial part of a microform should require permission
(5) Fair dealing procedures should be established for the production of eye-legible copies for study
(6) Special conditions for legal deposit of microforms should be introduced:
(a) copies of microforms constituting first publication of texts in in the U.K. should be offered for payment at cost to the British Library
(b) speculative editions of microforms should contribute a free copy to the British Library
(c) copies deposited should be of 'best material'
(7) All published microforms, whether deposited or not, should be notified to the British Library and entered in BNB or an equivalent.

712 One or two comments may be made on the points of MAGB's submission:
(a) protection as publications is preferred to protection as photographs
(b) protection sought for publishers' front matter is modest, and less than is now afforded by the 1956 Act, if by protection similar to that for typographic arrangement is implied a shorter period, e.g. of 25 years.

The Library Association

713 The LA's evidence made four special points on microforms:
(1) making original microforms, enlargements from microforms and duplication of microforms should all be regarded as making copies
(2) where a microform publication consists of more than one original

document, the copying of the complete text or a substantial part of one text should constitute an infringement

(3)   blanket licensing could be made a condition of the sale of microform duplicating machines

(4)   microform publishers should be required to submit copies of each item to national deposit bodies.

SCONUL also made the same point as the LA's No. 4, otherwise microtexts featured only slightly in the evidence to Whitford that we have seen.

Whitford Report

714   In the Whitford Report itself there are several mentions of microforms. It is recognised that there are differences of degree between ordinary publications and micro publications, and that publishing can be on an on-demand basis. Later the Report states, without making a formal recommendation of it, that a new copyright act 'should make it clear that microcopies are simply facsimile copies and that the relevant provisions apply accordingly. It will be open to the parties involved to negotiate special terms and conditions for this category of copying if this is thought to be appropriate'. The Committee's own opinion on publisher's protection from unauthorised copying of their microtexts is that it already exists as 'typographical arrangement' or 'published edition' protection under Section 15 of the 1956 Act for all 'micro-publications which are not merely copies of earlier editions', but they agree it should be made clearer.

715   Whitford's remaining mentions are about legal deposit. In discussing evidence received the Report reveals that the deposit libraries all thought microtexts should be included in deposit requirements; the MAGB's evidence is mentioned (see 711) concerning number of copies to be deposited, and definition of publication. Later the Report reminds us that the Gregory Committee also thought microtexts should be included in deposit obligation. The Whitford Committee think some clarification of publication may be necessary, but that it is necessary to tread warily in view of other copyright aspects. It will be noted that nowhere does the Whitford Report assume that micro-publications are protected as photographs, and remembering that the Whitford Committee had on it the principal legal authority on copyright, we must leave the reader to decide the matter for himself.

Audio visual materials

716   The special problems of copyright in non-textual works are of two main kinds: the multiplication of bodies that can have a copyright interest in a single format and the varied nature of the infringing acts, not necessarily including the reproduction of the original, that the user has to avoid. I do not intend to go into great detail about the Copyright Act 1956's provisions for all kinds of non-textual materials for two reasons: first because many of the copyright hazards set about tapes, broadcasts, etc., will not usually confront the librarian in his normal duties; and excellent explanations of the present state of the law have been published. I should especially mention the Council for Educational Technology (CET), which in 1972 under its former title the National Council for Educational Technology published *Copyright and education*. This was supplemented in 1976 by *Copyright and contract* and *Copyright clearance*, both by their Rights Development Officer, Geoffrey Crabb. *Copyright and education* is a statement of the law relating to copyright as it might affect the teacher, together with proposals for improvements, and a useful set of appendices of relevant documents. In the other two, Geoffrey Crabb shows the stages a teacher would need to go through to use copyright material without infringement, setting out an algorithm or flow chart covering all forms of material and all types of action, whether permitted or not, that he might wish to take with the material.

717   A further aid to the perplexed enquirer in these fields is available in Charles Gibbs Smith's pamphlet *Copyright law concerning works of art, photographs and the written and spoken word*, first published by the Museums Association in 1970, a slightly revised and expanded version coming out in 1974. The particular strengths of this work, apart from its reliability on matters of interpretation, are in the detailed treatment of artistic (visual) works (it does not deal with films, records, etc.) and its very clear, not to say emphatic expression. I commend the reader to these publications and here acknowledge my debt to them in understanding the law as it stands.

718   My purpose, then, is to foresee some of the problems that can confront a librarian in the course of his duties, and offer what guidance I can on the correct actions to take. It seems to me that there are certain specific areas of librarianship where copyright problems with audio-visual materials are most likely to arise: the music or record library; the local history or local studies department, and public library extension activities; and, of course, the school library, but first it would be advisable to deal with illustrative matter in books and other graphic materials that any department operating a photocopying or photographic service could have to deal with.

Illustrations

719   We have already seen (104, 296-7) that illustrations as parts of periodical articles may be copied under the Section 7 Regulations. This permission also extends to copying illustrations as part of extracts from books, provided of course that the inclusion of illustrations in

the extract does not thereby make the extract more than a substantial part, and provided that the illustrations form a true part of the extract. It should also be remembered that in the case of illustrations that are reproductions of artifacts (e.g. oil paintings) that may themselves be long out of copyright, copyright subsists in the photograph for fifty years after the end of the year of its first publication. A final warning is that there is a presupposition in favour of illustrations' copyright being infringed by copying since each one is usually a separate work.

Maps

720 One of the types of graphic publication that librarians are frequently asked to copy is maps. Whether these are part of an atlas or separate sheets, great care should be exercised. A part of a map in an atlas could probably be copied as not a substantial part, but it would be preferable to ask the publisher whether he would permit whole maps to be copied — frequently publishers are less restrictive than the law provides. In the case of single sheet maps, even those in a series, it would be a clear infringement to copy the whole, even a black and white copy of a coloured original. If there is no opportunity to obtain permission for copying parts of maps, the best advice would be to limit the copying to 10% of the whole by area.

721 The Ordnance Survey now allows libraries to copy 700 sq. cm. (just under $10\frac{1}{2}''$ x $10\frac{1}{2}''$) from any one map but offers licences for copying beyond that limit. See the statement in *A librarian's handbook, v.2* (1980) (ref. 16) for the full details. One matter on which the Ordnance Survey has been taken to task, but by the publishers rather than librarians, is the high rate of fee they charge for reproducing sections of maps, and there is the added complication that many details on large scale plans have remained the same for over fifty years and are therefore thought to be out of copyright. A publisher basing his own map exclusively on Ordnance Survey material published more than fifty years ago may claim exemption from fees, but so far the Ordnance Survey has taken a hard line against this pleading. However this should not deter the librarian asked for a photocopy — even of the whole of map published, whether by the Ordnance Survey or not, more than fifty years ago. It has by now no copyright protection.

Photographs

722 Some libraries make photographic prints instead of contact photocopies of graphic materials whether same size, reduced or enlarged, for their users, since the quality of the reproduction of small details (e.g. half-tones or lithographs) would be inadequate otherwise. It should be decided whether the library offering this service wishes to keep the copyright in these photographs, or transfer it to the user on supplying the copy. There will be a negative from which further prints can be

taken and the right to use this negative should be settled between the parties. Normally the copyright and the right to produce and issue further copies will belong to the customer, as the one who commissions the photograph; though he may not own the negative, the library can make no more prints without the copyright owner's consent. This is clearly an undesirable situation, and even though the library can extricate itself easily by taking another photograph and destroying the first negative, it is best avoided by a clear understanding at the start.

723   There are many libraries with collections of photographs, especially in local studies collections. Librarians should realise that under the 1956 Act until they are published, copyright subsists in them indefinitely, but after publication for fifty years. Photographs made before the 1956 Act came into force, 1st June 1957, are protected only for 50 years from the date they were made. Ownership of a photograph's copyright, however, is with the person who commissioned it to be taken. Possession of the negative does not presume ownership of the copyright and libraries wishing to make copies or prints from photographs in their possession would be well advised to establish where copyright ownership lies. They will be relieved, however, to discover that showing a photograph in an exhibition does not constitute publication, and is not a prohibited act, though to make an enlargement of a photograph for an exhibition or display, probably would be an infringement. There seems to be some doubt in this area and it has been said that since epidiascope showing of illustrations or photographs is not an infringement since no copy is made, making a slide for projection in the same way should not be regarded as an infringement either, especially as slide projectors have largely superseded epidiascopes. The difficulty is that the slide is a 'fixing' of the original and can be disposed of or used in other contexts. *Photocopying and the law* allows single copies of illustrative matter to be made for educational instruction in schools or colleges, provided an acknowledgement of the source is made. I take leave, however, to regard the making of slides from photographs as a potentially infringing act since it is creating a copy from an original. Certainly a copyright slide cannot be printed out as a photograph without permission.

724   Now that I have mentioned slides it should be noted that the copying of slides to make into filmstrips or the copying of filmstrip frames to make up individual slides would also be infringements, though these actions can be taken without copying. It is no infringement physically to break up a filmstrip and mount the frames as slides. The insertion of new matter into a published filmstrip or set of slides, however, should be done with caution, since although no copyright infringement takes place, the law against passing off the work of one as that of another could come into operation. Copies of artistic works may, however, be taken as fair dealing for the purposes of research or private study, and it is perhaps open to libraries to supply copies for these purposes, taking advantage of the protection in Section 9 of the 1956 Act (but see the discussion on fair dealing and libraries, 428-36). There are no accompanying regulations for this Section, but libraries would be well advised to secure declarations similar to those under Section 7, for their own safeguard. The context in which these acts might be contemplated could be a school library resource centre, or preparations for an exhibition. It should be noted that the special exceptions protecting aducation (Section 41) are not all extended to staff other than teachers, and if the resource centre is not at the school further limitations apply. See *Copyright and education* (ref. 11) for these conditions.

725 While on the subject of photographs, I can turn to the question of taking photographs of copyright objects for inclusion in a local studies collection. Many libraries commission photographers to provide pictures of buildings and structures and events in their locality. No infringement takes place of architectural copyright by any amount of photographing, though of course architectural plans and drawings have copyright as artistic works. Again sculptures fixed in a public place and decorative features outdoors may be freely photographed. Exhibits in a museum or art gallery may not be separately photographed, though they can feature in a general photograph of an exhibition without infringement.

Performances

726 Before going on to records, tapes and films it would be as well to deal with performances of literary, dramatic and musical works. In general, performance in public is an act restricted by copyright (Section 2(5) (c)). Librarians' involvement in performances include readings at story hours, play readings in literary classes, and music performances whether on instruments or by records at lunchtime recitals. The same restrictions apply to any adaptations of the works. Under Section 6(5) of the 1956 Act, recitation of reasonable extracts of a work is not an infringement (unless the performance is broadcast), but it seems that there is no protection in law for the children's librarian who reads the whole of a work or even, perhaps, a complete story from a collection. The legal criterion of whether a reading is an infringement is in the nature of the audience: if within a family circle or to a few invited friends there is no infringement, but a children's story hour is generally public and even if the story is read to a children's library club this would be no protection if membership of the club were open to all who wished to join. The position is of course absurd, and no publisher or author would dream of refusing permission for stories to be read freely in these circumstances. It seems to be one of those rare cases where an infringement occurs that is (usually) positively beneficial to the copyright owner, and therefore more honoured in the breach than the observance. Librarians are advised to ask for permissions only in cases of authors or publishers who are known for being litigious and blind to their own interests.

727   Play-readings as in dramatic clubs where virtually all those present are taking part in the performance are not an infringement, but if any other audience is present permission needs to be sought. No distinction is observed here between a reading and a full-scale performance, though again, extracts of non-substantial length would be permitted. Performances in or by schools are permitted provided the audience is composed only of people connected with the school, e.g. other teachers and pupils, but not parents or guardians.

728   It takes some deviousness to envisage occasions when librarians might infringe copyright by performing music, other than on records or tapes, which will be dealt with later, but one such could be the engagement of a pianist to accompany a silent film at a library film club. There would be an infringement if copyright music was used there. The reason for making such an obscure point is that in their wider public activities librarians need to be watchful in the matter of any use of copyright material.

729   While it is no offence to show a photograph or slide in a lecture or an exhibition, some care must be exercised in setting up filmstrips, tape-slide packages, or sequences of slides. There can be no infringement in showing a sequence of slides unconnected except by the speaker's narrative, but a pre-packed presentation may be a different matter, and librarians responsible, say, for setting up back-projection slide sequences in exhibitions — a common enough occurrence — should inspect them for conditions of use. When such materials are hired, there is an implied licence to perform, but there may be conditions in the hiring to limit the number of showings or the size of audience. Similarly contractual obligations may be incurred when materials are purchased. Certainly although occasional use in exhibitions or invited audience lectures may be regarded as fairly safe, librarians should avoid holding regular widely attended public sessions in which this type of material plays an important part, unless they have explicit permission to do so.

Sound recordings

730   There is an alarming leap in copyright complexity when one comes to talk of gramophone records, tapes, films and video recordings. I cannot hope to cover all the aspects of copyright in this space, but again will draw attention to dangers that librarians seem to face in using these materials. In what follows 'record' covers all formats of

audio recording except sound track on cinematographic film. To start with, making, performing and copying records, etc. are all potential infringements. To take making a record first, let us assume that a library sponsors an event or becoming aware of it, wishes to keep a permanent record of it. Such an event might be a recital, concert or dramatic performance, or perhaps a debate on its premises. Librarians should realise that copyright inheres not only in music, words to music, translations of the words, authorised arrangements of all three, plays and speeches, but also in the performances of them. These last are protected by the Performers Protection Acts of 1958 and 1963 and not by the Copyright Acts. Recordings of copyright music and accompanying words may be made without infringement if previous recordings of the same work have been put on retail sale (by anyone in the U.K.), provided the intending recorder notifies the copyright owner of his intention to do so, and that the new recording is to be put on sale. A fixed royalty of $6\frac{1}{4}\%$ of the retail selling price must be paid. Naturally the performers of the music must agree to (and perhaps be paid for) the recording. Musical works are catered for in this country by the Mechanical Rights Society Ltd., for which fees are collected by the Mechanical-Copyright Protection Society.

731 Performances of dramatic works are licensed by publishers, who in some cases appoint agents. If no agent's name is given in the acting edition of the play (if there is one) application should be made to the publisher. This will apply to readings from literary works that constitute more than reasonable extracts. In all these cases the performers' permissions for recording must also be secured. Copyright cannot subsist in unscripted speeches, but it is well to enquire in appropriate cases if the speaker was using detailed notes, in which case he has a claim to copyright. Strange to say, in cases where no copyright exists in unscripted speech or dialogue, it is created by and belongs to the person who 'fixes' it either by writing it down, recording it, or filming it.

732 From making records we turn to using them, and first to simple performance. To add to the authors' or composers' copyright, where present in the material on the record and the performers' protection we now have copyright in the recording itself: this lasts fifty years after first publication. To perform a record publicly then, a licence has to cover all these interests. In practice Phonographic Performance Ltd (PPL) acts as agents for virtually all record companies (the list as at c.1972 is on p.67 of *Copyright and education*). PPL distributes royalties agreed to record companies and artistes for the record copyright and the performance, but any original music still in copyright must be cleared with the Performing Rights Society Ltd. PPL waive their rights in the case of educational use in schools and colleges; and the 1956 Act (Section 12(7)(b)) provides that clubs or other organisations not established or conducted for profit may perform records if their objects are charitable or concerned with the advancement of religion, education or social welfare. A library could normally count itself such an organisation. Performance of records as background music in a music department, however, needs to be cleared. At present PPL ask no fees, but policies could change: there is no legal protection in the Copyright Act itself for this use. Certainly enquiries should be made for use of records as incidental music for plays, or at concerts of recorded music where charges are made for admission. At WEA classes, though fees are charged, performances would be covered by the law's exemption as they are officially educational. Care should however be taken over records containing copyright words or music.

733 Private study of records by headphones, in booths or carrels, is not an infringement, but public performances, e.g. by jukeboxes, need to be licensed. The librarian who hires out a hall to another body can in certain circumstances be held liable for copyright infringements committed by his lessee; but usually only if he had direct knowledge of the proposed performances or if he takes a fee for the use of the hall in excess of a nominal amount or defrayment of expenses.

734 The copying of records is naturally an infringement and apart from the general proviso (Section 49) that no infringement takes place unless a substantial part is copied, there is no protection for fair dealing for research or private study, nor for educational purposes. This is a great disadvantage as copies are wanted not for resale but for easier handling. It is permitted, for example, for a private individual to perform a gramophone record at home — naturally, this is the intention of selling it — but if he wishes to study a section in detail, he might find it more convenient to transfer that part onto a tape recording. This he may not do if it is more than a substantial part. A library record club, though permitted to perform recordings, could not for instance tape record a lengthy work on 78 r.p.m. discs merely to avoid the disruptive breaks in performance, erasing the tape afterwards, without acquiring permission first. The chances are that permission would be given, but frequently the inevitable delay would make the venture not worthwhile. The same applies to schools, where although it is permitted to to play the recording in class, it may not be put onto a tape for easier use. In the case of recordings already on tape, they may not be transferred to different speeds of tape, or onto any other format. However, Phonographic Performance Ltd does offer licences to educational institutions for these purposes. When looking for shelter under the protection that one is not copying a substantial part, it is worth remembering that in musical works a short theme could be considered a substantial part of a lengthy work.

735 The law is not primarily intended to prevent the reasonable acts we have been considering, but the copying of complete records, usually onto tape, from borrowed or shared originals for the copier to keep or dispose of as though they were authorised examples of the recordings. Libraries with record or tape lending sections should beware of encouraging this practice by their users, and they should probably include a warning against copyright infringement with every loan made. Mechanical-Copyright Protection Society, however, do offer licences to cover these acts. A library's liability in such a case of infringement is not clear, and perhaps it is not great, especially if it is not making a profit out of the record lending service, but a warning notice would add to its protection.

Cinematograph films

736 The same three actions: making, performing and copying, are all potential infringements in the case of cinematograph films. In making a film, there is the extra hazard that one may illegally copy an artistic work or incorporate a sound recording. Few libraries make their own films as yet but more and more activities involve videotape, and it is fairly clear that courts would regard videotape as a format of the same kind as cinematograph film, even though by a technicality (the mention in the 1956 Act of visual images) they are not strictly of the kind of materials explicitly protected as film (Whitford Report ref. 50, paras 887-9).

737 Some libraries have made films or videotapes of local events, in much the same way as records have been made. Extra points to note are that copyright works of art (except fixed sculptures and works of architecture) may not be the subject of individual attention in such films or tapes, though general views incorporating them, as in an exhibition, are permitted. Sound films may not include performances of copyright records. The rights of any literary or dramatic work performed in the process would be infringed only if 'a substantial number of detailed incidents are reproduced.' (ref. 3, p.306). One could take a film or videotape of a town carnival for example. The artistic copyright in any floats would be infringed by two-dimensional representation of a three-dimensioned object, since the objects are not permanently sited in public, and could not be said to be in the background or incidental, and the music performed by the bands and the performances of the bandsmen and others would still be protected. The filming or videotaping of the music and its performance could also be an infringement. In the face of all this, many would surely give up the idea.

738 Much the same considerations apply to films as to records in their performance. One may not show a film in public, or even it would would appear perform the sound track alone; one may not broadcast the film or relay it on a diffusion service. The only exceptions allowed

are performing it for judicial proceedings or as part of the activities of a school when performed by a teacher or pupil. This leaves a wide area of possible concern to librarians. Films are borrowed or bought for staff training, are acquired for stock, to be consulted on the premises (e.g. by means of an 'editor'), but only very rarely, in the UK, for general or public loan; they may however be shown at public performances, e.g. at conferences or library clubs if of special local relevance. The best guidance that can be given is that when hiring or purchasing films, the conditions of hire or sale should be carefully noted; they usually include conditions under which they may be performed. In many cases documentary films are made for publicity purposes and the widest showing is desired by the publisher without extra remuneration. Or a limit to the number of performances, in the case of a hired film, may be given, or a restriction on the size or type of audience, in the case of a purchased film. If admission is charged for this may vary the conditions of sale or hire. The important point is that all these performances are potential infringements unless cleared by the copyright owner through hire or sale: there is no defence in the copyright law.

739   One difficulty in performing films in school — and note that only schools, not colleges, are protected — is that performance must be by a teacher or pupil. Naturally most schools would prefer to employ a technician or projectionist if they have one, and in some instances these staff would come under the supervision of a librarian in a resource centre. The letter of the law would not permit this, though the defence that a projectionist was the teacher's or pupil's authorised agent might succeed. Here the school might in any case be protected by the terms on which the film was obtained: most hire and purchase charges include an element of royalty where the copyright owner requires it.

740   It is worth noting that the term of copyright in films is now 50 years after the end of the year of first publication. Before the 1956 Act films had no copyright as such but were protected as photographs, sound recordings, literary, dramatic works, etc, separately. Publication is defined a little differently in that the issue of copies for sale to the public is not the essential point; alternatively publication is established by the hire of copies, or the first announcement of availability of sale or hire. Naturally offences occur if the infringing acts are done before publication, the same as afterwards. A warning may be given here about infringing copies. Owing to the vast extent of the 'pirate' film industry, illegal copies of films: feature, documentary and even training — some of very good technical quality — are more likely than other media to find their way into innocent hands by way of trade or otherwise. Especial care should be taken to acquire or use only authorised copies.

741 When it comes to copying films there are no loopholes. Transferring a cinematograph film to videotape or a videotape to film are both reasonable acts: the first to facilitate showing and reduce damage through use to the original; and the second to preserve the length of life of the film, which though more subject to mechanical damage, lasts longer than a videotape which degenerates with use. But in both cases the copying would be an infringement. To transfer a nitrate film to a safety based film is even more desirable, and may still not be allowed, but there are probably comparatively few of these still in copyright.

742 The copying of extracts from tapes or films is protected by the general exemption of not copying a substantial part, but there may be extra dangers here, when extracts are incorporated into other productions, of distortion or parody, of the original. The exception for schools in Section 41 of the 1956 Act, though it covers performances of films, does not protect the making of copies of films. Librarians may make copies of extracts only of non-substantial parts: there is no protection in the fair dealing clause (Section 6) or the exemptions for libraries (Section 7).

Broadcasts

743 Finally in this round of audio-visual materials we come to the least 'material' form of all: the broadcast. Conditions of copyright are different again: broadcasts of sound or television by the broadcasting authorities are protected as broadcasts and their term of protection is fifty years, as usual, but this dates only from the 1956 Act. Broadcasts made before the Act came into force (i.e. 1st June 1957) are without copyright protection, unless re-broadcast. So one's freedom is limited to copies made from the earlier occasion. Once a re-broadcast of an earlier item is made, its protection lasts fifty years from the time of the first re-broadcast.

744 The acts in which the librarian is interested are here only those of performing and copying. He may have no copyright interest in his own broadcasts since protection is afforded only to the main broadcasting authorities. Performance of a television broadcast in public is permitted in a library or any other place provided admission charges are not made or service charges for any other goods increased because of the broadcast. This allows live broadcasts to be seen, for example, at club evenings, or during library opening hours. The proviso against the paying audience is not applicable to sound broadcasts, but it is hard to think of an example where this extra relaxation could benefit libraries. The paying audience is still admissible for protection where the television broadcast is made as part of the general facilities of a club, or where persons are normally resident, but this again will rarely arise in library circumstances. Recording a broadcast, either on sound or film, is a more restricted act. It may be done 'for private purposes,' but I have found no suggestion that this may done by a library for generalised private use, or even for supply to an individual user.

745   What is more important to remember, however, is that broadcasts are protected only as broadcasts: any copyright material contained in them is separately protected, and it would be an infringement to record even for private use a broadcast gramophone record or film. And although artistic works are not infringed by television broadcasting provided their inclusion is only incidental to the broadcast, literary, dramatic and musical rights are infringed by inclusion in a broadcast, as also is the right of typographic arrangement.

746   Schools are protected in a small but important measure, outside the copyright law, by an arrangement with the BBC and ITV, under which programmes broadcast specifically for schools, and no others, may be recorded in the school for later and repeated use, provided the recordings are destroyed no later than one year after being made (three years after for radiovision programmes). This licensing arrangement includes recording from copyright gramophone records included in the broadcast, but teachers may not record the same work (even the same recording) from a copy in their possession: the licence is for the broadcast only. Unfortunately for librarians, no such arrangements exist even for schools in the case of Open University programmes. The sensible and useful proposal by some libraries to record Open University programmes off air and make them available on library premises for individuals or groups to study at other times has not been possible to arrange, because of contractual difficulties over copyright and performers' rights.

747   Thus far the law as it stands on audio-visual materials. Going back to 1972, and the NCET's booklet *Copyright and education*, we find some of the reasonable objections to the law made by teachers. In the section 'What the teacher wants to do', NCET first calls for general clearance procedures to cut out the multiple applications for permission that are now necessary. 'The basic demand from the classroom', they say, 'is for the production, at short notice, of enough material to meet the needs of the students.' The development of resource centres with specialist staff makes it easier technically for schools to employ various kinds of materials in education. The detailed provisions of the copyright act make it no simpler to apply for many permissions at once than one at a time, and for a thorough-going exploitation of audio-visual materials, staff would be continuously engaged in correspondence with copyright proprietors.

748   Librarians acting as agents for teachers in schools and colleges have

the same interest in campaigning for simpler formalities or their abolition. In their booklet NCET put forward three possible courses of action: (1) extend educational exceptions in the copyright act, not forgetting that the Performers Protection Acts would also need amending, (2) charge for certain recreational uses in the price of the materials, (3) encourage negotiated agreements between users and copyright owners, so that blanket permissions for certain actions could be held by schools and colleges. In seeing possible progress in the third of these, NCET suggests that the establishment of a central body able to negotiate for all educational users and a central licensing body for the copyright owners in various media would be the most wished-for first steps. That NCET would have been ready to step into the new shoes of the first of these bodies can hardly be doubted.

749 Certainly librarians would also welcome simplified ways of clearing use of copyright audio-visual material, but they might be more chary of becoming involved with licensing and negotiating bodies. Their users' needs at present rarely call for intensive or extensive performance or copying of graphic, sound or moving picture materials, unless we include those schools and colleges where library staff are heavily involved in resource centre technicalities. Most librarians would take the view that fair use exceptions should cover the infrequent occasions when they need to transfer a record to tape, or copy a television programme for local reasons, for example. To this proposition copyright proprietors would react with 'thin end of the wedge' arguments, and pointing to what has happened with print copying, could reasonably claim that technical improvements/developments would rapidly encourage all parties to make more and more copies for more and more reasons to supply to more and more users.

Whitford Committee evidence : The Library Association

750 The Whitford Committee was specifically instructed to examine the problem of taping audio records and cassettes, but this was hardly a library problem, except insofar as libraries frequently operated record and cassette lending libraries. The offences were believed to occur mostly in private houses. The Library Association's evidence to the Whitford Committee recommended that 'the same principles should apply to audio-visual as to conventional printed materials', while admitting that the materials need special treatment, and supporting the CET's efforts in arranging blanket licences. Four specific points were made:

(1) fair dealing to cover personalised learning is needed
(2) educational exemptions should be extended from schools to colleges and universities, and to their libraries
(3) when permissions are required for making copies, this should be by blanket licence
(4) library or resource centre staff should be permitted to make fair dealing copies for educational institutions.

Council for Educational Technology

751 The CET in its evidence to the Whitford Committee made the following recommendations:

(1) copyright and performers' rights should continue to be protected

(2) all educational institutions should be free to make what copies they need, within fair limits, without needing to seek prior permission

(3) educational concessions must be clearly expressed

(4) the benefits of various types of institution should be clearly differentiated

(5) there must be arrangements to cater for changing needs and technical facilities

(6) detailed accounts of copying should not need to be maintained by educational institutions

(7) five systems to achieve the Council's objectives could be considered:
   (a) levy on equipment
   (b) remuneration from central government
   (c) levy on consumables in copying
   (d) extension of educational exemptions
   (e) extension of fair dealing

(8) if fair dealing was extended, rights owners could corporately define its limits in various fields

(9) negotiated blanket licences should cover the educational users for copying beyond those limits

(10) an arbitration body to decide what was fair dealing or what was a suitable licence would be needed in cases of dispute

(11) the CET favours the fair dealing extension, but recognises the advantage of a levy on equipment

(12) a body should be set up involving rights owners and educational users to reconcile their possibly conflicting interests. CET itself would offer its good offices to create the basis of such a body.

Publishers' Association

752 The PA had little to say in its lengthy evidence about audio-visual materials, but it did comment on the inadequacy of closed-circuit television arrangements in the current law. The confusion over whether such systems were broadcasts or diffusion services created undesirable contradictions. I have not discussed CCTV in the section on the law on audio-visual materials, since it seems unlikely to occur in library situations. The PA's concern was the possibility of using CCTV to substitute for purchases of sufficient copies of published items, and of avoiding paying a compensatory fee for such use.

Standing Conference of National and University Libraries

753 SCONUL recognised the value of the work done by CET, but added the following to its evidence:

(1) copying for creating and disseminating audio-visual materials should be permitted under fair dealing rules

(2) negotiated arrangements for use of materials should improve access for study purposes

(3) levies on recording equipment could be unfair to libraries which have for many years provided a service that prejudiced no-one

(4) BBC general programmes are of increasing value for education: permission to use them under the same conditions as specifically educational broadcasts would be a considerable benefit
(5) the one year rule on erasing recorded broadcasts should be re-examined
(6) legal deposit should be introduced for audio-visual materials.

Whitford Report

754 The Whitford Report has a comparatively short section (41 paragraphs in 10 pages) on audio and visual recording, but this is supplemented by chapters on statutory recording licence, performing rights and performers' rights, and diffusion. Dealing first with audio and video recording the Report recognises that audio recording is already operating at a high level (45% of homes have access to a facility, and 20% of people over 16 have at some time recorded from commercial records or tapes, according to a 1975 survey), and that video recording is increasing. Much of the copying is done privately. The Report then sets out briefly the present legal position and refers to existing licensing schemes. Discussion of the international scene brings in a description of the German levy system on recording equipment. In recounting the evidence they have received, the Committee refer to various suggestions that the German system should be introduced, or that fair dealing should be extended. The CET's evidence (751) is dealt with in detail, and mention is made of the special problems that are said to face further education in scheduling classes to make best use of broadcast programmes that may not be copied as non-specifically educational.

755 The Report presents as the Committee's conclusions the following points:

(1) the only possible solution to recording problems lies in blanket licensing levy or by negotiation
(2) fair dealing should not be extended to non-literary works since a reasonable level would not satisfy most users, and a widening of fair dealing's scope would be unfair to copyright owners
(3) private recording should be catered for by a levy on equipment, and not on tapes, etc.
(4) collecting societies should be designated by the Minister, and a statutory tribunal should decide rates of levy and distribution of its proceeds
(5) for educational use, the levy on equipment purchased should be supplemented by an annual fee paid under a blanket licence scheme
(6) blanket licensing should be generally patterned on the proposals for reprography (see 525)
(7) performance by educational establishments of recorded materials should be permitted under Section 41 of the 1956 Act, but performances to wider audiences would need to be negotiated with collecting societies
(8) these proposals relate to non-commercial use: commercial use should still be subject to normal licensing arrangements
(9) existing equipment should be free to operate under these proposals as soon as they are put into effect, without a fee being paid on them.

756 Looked at in the light of libraries' interests, the tenor of these proposals
is quite at variance with that of the proposals on reprography. There
the attitude was that libraries must be prevented from driving publishers
out of business, by charging them for every copy they make. Here
libraries are ignored and certainly not seen as a special threat. The
reason, I believe, lies in a sentence of the Whitford Report, 'We have
received no evidence that the problem of non-commercial recording
exists to any very appreciable extent outside the field of education
and private use.' So for a once only payment on new equipment
libraries could do a multitude of things not now permitted. Of course
we have still to discover what that equipment levy might be, but
Whitford refers approvingly to the German system, and that has a
percentage at present not exceeding 5%, though an application has
been made to increase it. And of course, this will apply only to new
purchases; old or borrowed equipment would be freely usable.

Educational institutions

757 In the case of libraries of educational institutions, an annual licence
fee would also have to be paid, and this is an unknown factor, but I
venture to think even that might be welcomed, when the advantages
of free copying within 'non-commercial' lines are considered. Here are
some of the actions that librarians could well be permitted:

(1) the transfer of materials from one medium to another (from record
to tape, from film to video, etc.)
(2) the supply to users of extracts from records, tapes and films
(3) the supply to users of complete copies of out of print records, tapes
and films
(4) the copying of any materials in stock for preservation purposes
(5) the recording off air of sound or television broadcasts for future use,
whether by designation educational or not, and whether or not they
incorporated other copyright materials.

Should the Whitford Report's recommendations come into force, it is
hard to imagine that other libraries would not join educational institutions in being required to pay an annual licence fee for such privileges.
The use of audio and video recordings and their varied exploitation
can surely only increase. Here is an illustration of the gradual and
empirical development of the copyright laws, which expand to cover
new uses only as those uses become more regular, and therefore more
of a threat. The Whitford Committee has failed to see the threat to
audio-visual materials from library copying.

Statutory recording licence

758 Going on to Chapter 6, Statutory Recording Licence, under which
musical works in copyright may be recorded subject to payment of a
standard royalty, the Whitford Committee propose only changes of
detail, which are unlikely to involve libraries.

Performing rights

759 In Chapter 7, performing rights, dealt with under the Copyright Acts, and performers' rights, covered by the Performers' Protection Acts 1958 to 1972, are both considered. There are three points in the Whitford Committee's recommendations that are of importance for librarians. First they say Section 12(7) of the 1956 Act should be deleted. This is the clause (see 732) which permits the performance of sound recordings in clubs or other non-profit organisations. The Committee think this exception is an anomaly, and open to abuse; they cite cases to illustrate the difficulties that can arise. Any special provision, say for charitable organisations to perform records can, they say, be negotiated by licence. A further limitation, which only a majority of the Committee wish to introduce, is that when a broadcast is caused to be heard in a public place, it should be an infringement if a copyright sound recording is broadcast by this means. These two restrictions would require libraries to take out licences from Phonographic Performance Ltd. if they wish either to run recorded music circles, or make publicly available television or sound broadcasts as part of their services.

Performers' rights

760 The third point concerns the continued protection of performers' rights. The Report refers to the CET's evidence that 'performers were able to negotiate contracts which would prevent the granting of reproduction rights to educational users even though the record companies, broadcasters and other rights owners were otherwise agreeable. The Musicians' Union, on the other hand said that though contracts whereby performers may prevent the granting of reproduction rights to educational users are unusual, there is no reason why they should not be free to make such a bargain'. The Whitford Committee here decided that performers' protection should not be reduced and made no amending recommendation. They do, however, refer to their blanket licensing system for educational recording. Presumably it will be up to the record company's agents, usually Phonographic Performance Ltd., to negotiate with each set of performers when making educational licences instead of being able to devote a standard proportion of the proceeds of the licence to the performers' representatives without negotiation. These difficulties would affect libraries if, as I suspect, they are required to take annual licences for the use of audio and video recording (755-7) in addition to paying a levy on the purchase of their equipment. The final chapter, no. 8, on diffusion, among those in the Whitford Report on audio-visual materials, contains no matters that have any bearing I can discern on library activities.

Legal deposit

761 In chapter 18 on libraries of legal deposit, the Committee, who are generally of the opinion that legal deposit is not a part of copyright, and therefore refrain from making positive recommendations on the subject, note that for audio-visual materials the question of establishing a national archive could give rise to different problems from those to do with printed matter. They note that the deposit libraries are not equipped to assume the additional burden, and the existing national bodies — the British Institute of Recorded Sound and the British Film Institute — operate on a rather modest scale at present. It could, they think, be a large undertaking, and the subject needs further investigation.

Responses to Whitford Report

762 It is now necessary to see what reactions have been made to these recommendations. The opinions of the CET are those that carry most weight, but first, a look at some other organisations' responses. The Library Association was so concerned about the reprographic proposals that it made no mention of audio-visual materials in its response to the Report. SCONUL, however, was reluctant to accept a levy on the sale of equipment and the supplementary blanket licence for educational institutions. If levels of charging were to justify the expense of collection they would be set so high as to be a 'serious deterrent to the use of such material'. SCONUL urged the extension of fair dealing and educational exceptions to recording for private study and research and to small group teaching.

University of London Library Resources Co-ordinating Committee

763 The University, in a lengthy statement, has three paragraphs on 'non-book materials'. It makes these points:

(1) a royalty on the sale of recording equipment is reasonable
(2) the educational exceptions (Section 41), which it is not proposed to extend to all educational users, should be so extended
(3) support is given to CET's proposal for reducing the power of the Performers' Protection Acts
(4) diffusion of pre-recorded broadcasts could be important, but the proposals for educational recording would cover educational users
(5) the restriction on rediffusion broadcasts to the time of original transmission is grudging — licences are recommended for other arrangements and for diffusing materials from non-broadcasting authorities
(6) 'school' needs to be redefined to cover all educational institutions
(7) the need to seek permission for reproduction of photographs is a hindrance to teaching, e.g. where slide preparation for lectures is involved.

Royal Society

764 The Society had some remarks on maps and photographs. It called attention to the confusion between the use of information contained on a map and reproduction of the map or a portion of it. The fact that much Ordnance Survey current map content is of old origin weakens the claim by the Survey and endorsed by the Whitford Committee that such is the work involved in map making that even a small area of a map could be a substantial part when copied. It also remarked that the Ordnance Survey collects some of its information from other sources (see 721). The Royal Society's point on photographs concerned aerial photographs. It is of the opinion that for the author and copyright owner of a photograph to be defined as the person responsible for the composition of the photograph is inadequate for aerial photographs. It also reminds the Department that data may be extracted from photographs without copyright infringement.

Council for Educational Technology

765 Finally in this chapter we have the reactions to the Whitford Report of the CET on matters concerning audio-visual materials. It:

(1) supports a negotiated blanket licensing scheme for audio and video recording

(2) opposes payment of a levy on equipment for educational users: suggests this could be reclaimed

(3) is concerned at the decision not to include performers' rights in the obligatory arrangements for recording; the Council's experience is that the Musicians' Union is reluctant to permit recordings to be made, and it cannot understand why the Committee accepted its plea that performers' rights should be preserved in this area

(4) notes that the distinction between schools and other educational institutions is preserved by the Committee in the matter of performance, though not in the matter of recording. The effect would be for colleges and universities to be allowed to record tapes, programmes, etc., but not to perform them in instructional situations; urges that the new act should allow performances of all materials in educational curricular use, whether from licensed copies or otherwise

(5) on the proposed abolition of Section 12(7) (see 759) the Council thinks it pointless to impose an obligation on sound recordings makers to permit re-recording while removing from some classes of user (including educational) an existing concession that allows them to be performed. The concession (in Section 40(1)) applies to hotels and social service organisations as well as education, and the Committee apparently sees no distinction between them

(6) subject to its proviso about recording under licence (see item 3 above) the Council supports the modification proposed on the Performers' Protection Acts (not dealt with above, as irrelevant to library interests)

(7) on diffusion, supports the proposal to extend coverage to sound recording and broadcasts, but opposes the restriction of educational exemption to that in Section 40(3) to 40(5) (effectively only to schools), and wishes to see exemption extended to all educational systems (effectively covering any arrangement with an education or training authority)

(8) the proposal that video recordings be included in the definition of cinematograph films is welcomed.

766 The general conclusions of the CET statement are particularly well expressed and pertinent: a bald summary would not do them justice, so I reproduce the final paragraph in full:

> "The Council welcomes the acceptance by the Committee that education should have the right to use protected material in various ways coupled with an obligation to pay equitable remuneration to the copyright owner. It welcomes the practical approach of the Committee and its recognition of current practices in education. It considers the schemes for statutory licensing to be sensible, but is concerned that higher and further education will, in the areas of diffusion and performance, be less well provided for than under the 1956 Act. In particular the Council feels that the Committee may have been too reluctant to think outside the confines of the existing legislation and too ready to equate educational, and especially higher and further educational, use with non-educational use. The Council sympathises with the wish to restrict the number of exceptions but, for example, to extend to education and training generally the right to perform as presently granted to schools, is not to increase the exceptions but only rationalise an existing one. In particular, there is a tendency to separate 'schools' from education generally. This is an increasingly artificial distinction in view of the development of sixth form and tertiary colleges, the introduction of the Open University, and the increasing number of open and distant learning systems in which the student learns under the guidance of staff in an educational institution but may not be physically present in the institution for much of the duration of the course. The Council considers that concessions should relate to the process of education and training and not be tied to particular classes of establishment which, over the period of the new act may change or even disappear."

While this is an admirable statement of the legitimate interests of education, one has only to read it with libraries in mind to realise that it is capable of logical extension.

Computers

767   There is probably no need to go far back in time to discuss the source of current problems of copyright to do with computers. I shall be looking principally at the Whitford Report's conclusions and reactions to them, and the new American copyright law (which receives closer attention in the next chapter), and the deliberations of the American body CONTU, the National Commission on the New Technological Uses of Copyright Works. A rather fuller discussion is found in Colin Tapper's book (ref 91a). The scope of this brief enquiry will be over the following activities:

(1)   the creation of copyright works by computer
(2)   the use of copyright works in a computer
(3)   the protection of computer programs or instructions.

Computer-created works

768   Although computers were a new phenomenon in the copyright world, and neither the Gregory Committee nor the 1956 Act contained any reference to them, the Whitford Committee were concerned to treat their processes and products as far as possible according to precedents set by the law relating to other activities and forms of material already recognised. Thus in the case of works produced by computer operations, the Committee regarded them as literary or artistic works, provided the amount of skill and/or labour that went into their preparation justified their being regarded as works. Thus digitised maps, programs compiled by a computer, computer aided design, or abstract music, can all be computer products and will have a claim to copyright. The owner of the copyright will be the person or persons responsible for the data and programming instructions used. The Committee recognise that this will frequently involve two or more parties, and therefore say such works should be regarded as of joint authorship. The term of copyright should be the same as for other literary, artistic and musical works, fifty years after the end of the year of death of the last author to die. The Committee are not breaking any new ground here, and so the usual conditions of authorship will apply, of which the most important will be whether the work is made under a contract of service or employment or is a commissioned work.

769   Librarians need, then, to beware of copying any computer products since they are probably protected as original productions or as adaptations. Even a meaningless compilation produced for study purposes or an analytical work, such as a list in alphabetical order of the words in Shakespeare's sonnets, or a concordance to the Bible may not be copied without permission, since although the data (the texts of works) are out of copyright, the program responsible for making the adaptation or rearrangement is not.

Computer software

770   Most of the time given by the Whitford Committee to computers was on the question of copyright in programs or software. Again, without invoking any new principle, they give their view that compilers of programs of all kinds are entitled to protection under copyright, whether that program is expressed in higher language, machine language or in accompanying matter such as user manuals or lists of instructions, and whether the program is readable, or on paper tape, or magnetic tape or any other medium. The present law, since there have been no cases, may or may not provide this protection. The Committee dismiss the notion of protecting programs by patent, referring to the recommendation of the Banks Committee in its 1970 report on the British patent system. They also feel that no special category of material need be created to protect computer programs: 'the only amendment necessary (to the law) is to make it clear that copyright subsists in any work recorded in such a way that it can be reproduced . . . whether in written form or as a recording or otherwise'.

771   In the United States the same problems have been exercising the minds of programmers, users and legislators, during the lengthy passage of the new Copyright Law. A survey in 1977 for CONTU showed that a variety of means of protection was in use among 'software houses' and other computer companies. These methods included patenting (6%), copyright (33%), trade secret law (35%), the need for 'know-how' (22%), cryptographic protection (6%) and other means to limit access to the software (29%), and this variety was reflected in earlier evidence at a CONTU meeting in 1976 that copyright was far from the only way of ensuring needed extra protection against abuse of rights in programs. However, CONTU did decide that programs were protected under the new law as 'works of authorship'. One CONTU member who dissented was the novelist John Hersey, who claimed that programs were writings of an author up to a certain point, beyond which they were embodied in material form and became mechanical devices. He saw the solution to the problem of giving copyright protection to machine instructions, in creating a computer software register (ref. 85). However, not satisfied with CONTU's view that the 1976 law protected programs, the Association of Data Processing Service Organisations Inc. (ADAPSO) urged CONTU not to strengthen one form of protection at the expense of others.

Restricted acts

772   Reverting to the Whitford Committee's deliberations, they next considered what acts should be restricted. The usual restricted acts for literary etc. works, are reproducing the work or an adaptation in any material form; publishing it for an adaptation; and making an adaptation. Publication of programs, though rare, may be encouraged by copyright protection being offered and secrecy discouraged, but the crux of the matter is the nature of 'reproducing' that would be restricted. After some discussion, the Committee make a majority decision that any handling of a program in a computer, including inputting it, involves a reproduction, and should therefore be a restricted act.

773   Should this provision find its way into law, librarians would need to be sure that programs offered them for computer services were not restricted from use: in other words that no 'black market' items were employed on their work. However, having got his computer, a 'clean' program, is a librarian justified in manipulating whatever data he wishes to produce lists, to search for categories of information and the like? The answer according to the Whitford Committee is, probably not. If the material providing the data or input is out of copyright there is of course no problem. But the Committee consider that inputting a copyright work into a computer is an act of copying and potentially an infringement, regardless of what use is made of it.

Computer handling

774   Although many general books carry a warning that 'no part of this publication may be reproduced, stored in a retrieval system, or transmitted, in any form or by any means, electronic, mechanical, photocopying, recording or otherwise, without the prior consent of the publishers,' and although such 'frighteners' may be effective in preventing photocopying, only rarely will normal readable texts be suitable for computer handling, which requires systematised matter before much can be made of it. The most likely matter to be input is bibliographies, indexes and abstracts with usable tags, and divisible into segments or fields of data. Without such arrangements computers can rarely do more than inspect separate words or phrases.

Abstracts and indexes

775   But index and abstract publishers are alert to the commercial value of their products as raw material for computer handling. Many have already arranged for computer tapes to be produced, together with standardised searching programs. These were in earlier years sold widely to organisations having their own computers, but the tendency now is to lease them to agents, or brokers, who then provide services on-line or by batch processing to their customers from a wider variety of data bases than any one publisher offers. This trend is likely to become intensified when the EURONET system becomes operational. Consequently, publishers of this type of material would be likely to lose a number of their normal customers as computer facilities, especially on-line, developed. At first computer charges could be low enough for libraries to retain their subscriptions to hard copies, but as computer charges increased, provided services remained reliable, there would be a temptation to dispense with the originals. No publisher that was careless in his computer leasing contracts would long survive. (see 916).

776   Cases have occurred of libraries or information centres making their own data base by merging sections of several separately published indexes or abstracts, perhaps adding to it from internal monograph additions lists. Whether this was an infringement would depend on the substantiality of the part taken from each original. If substantial, permission should be sought. Such cases would arise when the library either needed only small parts of very large data bases, or needed to search minutely, perhaps adding search facilities not in the package offered by the publishers or their agents. But once such a proceeding was legal, the library or information centre would have a new copyright in the merged data and in any printout from it. The question of copyright in printout from a data base is again settled by analogy with other materials. Copyright would subsist in such a product and would belong to the owner of the copyright data base, subject to any variation in format or content occasioned by the use of a particular program, in which case the program copyright owner would have a joint authorship copyright.

Substantiality

777 The question of substantiality, however, does give one pause. Normally, a print-out consisting of only a handful of references from a large data base — say of several thousand items — would seem a not substantial part. But if use of the data base is in question, it could be that the print-out is the result of scanning the whole content. It seems doubtful that scanning without printing out would constitute a reproduction of the original data in any sense intended by the Whitford Committee, and I should think copyright infringement in printout would depend on its substantiality. The further question of whether substantiality depends on quantity or quality is more difficult to settle. A short list comprising all the references on a specific topic from a broad subject data base might be considered substantial. The solution to such problems surely lies in contractual arrangements whereby input of or access to computerised data bases incorporates whatever printouts are available.

778 Compilers of library catalogues might worry if their input of authors and titles is an infringement. We have seen there is no copyright in titles, and copying these simple labels for cataloguing would be no infringement. However, to take one's cataloguing data exclusively from the *BNB*, say, using descriptive details, class marks, feature headings etc. more or less fully, and inputting it into one's own computerised catalogue would probably be an infringement, and permission should be sought. The availability of BLAISE services, however, makes compilations of this kind unlikely.

Responses to Whitford Report on Computers

779 Some comments have been made on the Whitford Committee's recommendations on computers. The CET supports the Committee's majority view that use of a program should be a restricted act, and also approves of the other recommendations. SCONUL says that the use of bibliographic data in machine readable form will require special consideration and treatment.

University of London Library Resources Co-ordinating Committee

780 The University has a lengthy section in its comments, making the following points:

(1) in general it agrees with the protection by copyright of computer programs, but

(2) there is insufficient protection for the originality of the principles

on which a program may be based. The analogy is made of a translation of a book, which requires permission though it is not a direct copy

(3)   the question of copying a principle of a computer program is again raised in comments on the difficulty of deciding whether a substantial part has been copied. The dangers are said to be strongest in new areas such as micro-computers, since in well-known fields the principles used are rarely original

(4)   in university systems, there may be abuse of copyright materials by users who are entitled to use the equipment, but who are not controlled in the programs they use by the computer centres. The difficulty of enumerating the forms in which computer programs may exist adds to this problem

(5)   the Committee's remarks on the importance of protecting adaptations of programs do not take account of essential mechanical steps in computer working, by which programs are converted

(6)   the relevance of data base compilation to the problem of privacy of information is noted; data bases may be easier to copy than to use

(7)   the Committee's difficulties over deciding whether input of data is reproduction are discounted; all input of copyright data would be a potential infringement.

In its introductory remarks the University compliments the Committee on the way it has coped with the problem of computers, 'a subject so deeply hidden in its own language and symbolism'.

Royal Society

781   The Society is less impressed. It emphasises the Whitford Committee's statement that the computer should be regarded as 'a mere tool in much the same way as a slide rule', and disagrees with the recommendation that copyright protection be extended to computer programs or the input of data, particularly statistical data and maps. Protection for the latter should be limited to copying for public use. This, it thinks, is what the Committee intended, but is not made clear in the Report. In this latter context it is interesting to note an American paper of 1975 by Belle L. Linden (ref. 87), in which copyright owners are represented as arguing 'that if copyright controls were imposed only at output, no compensation would be paid for the use of copyright materials which are never reproduced in replicative output but are manipulated, scanned, or similarly utilised within the computer.' On the face of it, if no copyright protection attached to inputting data, a data base agent or broker need pay nothing for his stock in trade, and would possibly find it more economical to keyboard afresh from the printed version than pay the rate for a tape from the publisher. In this way the only benefit the copyright owner would gain would be from printouts made possible by a third party — say a library or information centre serving its clients.

Patents

782   The brief reference above (770) to patenting computer software is an excuse for dealing with a small point raised by the Whitford Committee. A patent is a monopoly to use or lease a new device or invention exclusively for a limited period of time. Non-use invalidates it since it is created for the public good: a rather different attitude from that of copyright. It has been argued that when a patent expires, there is still a copyright in any drawings incorporated in a patent specification. This the Whitford Committee think undesirable and propose that there should be no copyright in expired patents. It should be noted that the 1977 Patents Act extended the maximum duration of a patent from 16 years (mentioned by the Whitford Report) to 20 years. As for the specifications during their term of validity, copyright has been said to vest in the Crown, as all publications put out by Government are Crown copyright, but since there are satisfactory copying services from the Science Reference Library for patent specifications, the question is not likely to arise very frequently.

Design protection

783   At this point it would be appropriate to mention other forms of protection akin to copyright that the law provides for designers and manufacturers. Design registration was covered by the Registered Designs Act of 1949. By this the outward appearance of an article is protected, not, as in patents, any principle or invention it incorporates. The protection is for objects for which copyright protection is not available, and includes manufactured articles of which more than 50 copies are produced, typically textile patterns. Design registration, which follows a procedure similar to patenting, gives the holder a monopoly in the use of the design for a maximum of fifteen years in three periods of five years. In 1968 the Design Copyright Act was passed, which supplements design registration, giving protection to industrially applied designs that are excluded from coverage by the Copyright Act 1956 and based on drawings that are not registered. Again the period of protection is fifteen years. It was partly to assess the success of the Design Copyright Act of 1968 that the Whitford Committee was set up. However, their recommendations were complex, and as the subject cannot be seen to have any close bearing on library problems, I do not propose to into them. For those who wish to study the subject of design protection in general, I recommend Dan Johnston's *Design protection* (ref. 86), a brief and clear exposition of the present position including trade marks and symbols, and the law of passing off, with a round-up of development overseas.

8
Copyright in the United States and Some Other Overseas Countries

United States

801   In a book designed as far as possible to be of practical use, an account of the main features of the United States copyright law is put in not to suggest how British librarians should deal with American works — the answer to that should be, in the same way as with British works — nor is it simply of academic interest. The United States has recently, after a long gestation, produced a full revision of its copyright law, and the detailed provisions for librarians and educators should give us useful thoughts about the best solutions to our problems, and an inkling of what our own legislators may have in store for us following the Whitford Report. And if a new Copyright Bill should come out that is less generous to our profession than the American law, then we shall be better armed with arguments to influence its passage through Parliament, by studying American experience.

802   There is no space here to recount the many revisions of text that preceded the final law, known variously as S.22 (its Senate numbering) and finally as Public Law (PL) 94-553. No doubt the arguments for and against the Williams & Wilkins case (1968-74, see 602-7) had some influence on its general favourability to the user, compared with the sterner attitude of the Whitford Committee. The text of the law is lengthy, and since there had been no general revision of copyright law since 1909, some measures to bring the United States into line with international conventions had to be included. I wish to concentrate in this brief account on matters affecting libraries, but it should also be noticed that some other important changes occurred. First the term of copyright was changed to life of the author plus fifty years, from 56 years after publication in two terms of 28 years. Transitional measures are required to effect this change, giving all productions before the law takes effect a period of 75 years of protection. The law was passed in October 1976, and came into force on 1st January 1978. Another general effect of the new law is that unpublished works are

protected by Federal, instead of simply State common law. The manufacturing clause, denying US copyright protection to works of US authors unless printed in the US is repealed, but not until July 1st 1982 (except for Canada where it took effect with the rest of law in 1978). Cable television and jukebox operation are now covered by copyright. A copyright royalty tribunal is to be set up to deal with disputes.

803   The law is in eight main sections:

(1) subject matter and scope of copyright (including exceptions for libraries etc.)
(2) copyright ownership and transfer
(3) duration of copyright
(4) copyright notice, deposit and registration
(5) copyright infringement and remedies
(6) manufacturing requirement and importation
(7) copyright office
(8) copyright royalty tribunal.

In the first section, which is the longest and the one most relevant to libraries, there are 18 sub-sections numbered 101-118. We shall be looking at sections 105, 106, 107 and 108 in some detail, but should note first that 101 comprises definitions of crucial terms, 102 defines the types of works for which authorship is attributable, 103 notes the restricted copyright available to compilations and derivative works, and 104 defines the conditions of nationality under which copyright protection is available, e.g. to nationals of countries that are parties to the Universal Copyright Convention.

Government publications

804   Section 105 states that US government publications are not protected by copyright, but that the government can hold copyrights assigned or bequeathed to it. This makes no change in US practice, and it has been well enough known in the UK that US government publications are not protected. The practice among libraries has generally been that copying is done freely of such works. This goes against the general conditions of international conventions, in that because UK government publications are protected by copyright, British users ought to give overseas publications the same treatment as their own. One can imagine the Stationery Office being concerned if their publications were 'pirated' in the US on the strength of this reciprocity. However, it has been made clear that publications put out by other bodies that arise from grants made by the US government are not free of copyright. This applies to the USGRDR lists (United States Government Research and Development Reports), which are distributed in standardised format (quarto and microfiche) by the NTIS (National Technical Information Service) in the US, and by their agents (currently Microinfo and the BLLD) in the UK. One recalls that

BLLD has replaced its policy of distribution of retention microfiches of these reports by a policy of lending microfiches or hard copies.

Exclusive rights

805 Section 106 lists the exclusive rights in copyrighted works that the law confers. They are, briefly, to reproduce the work in copies or on records; to prepare derivative works, to distribute copies or records to the public, to perform the work publicly, and to display the work publicly.

Fair use

806 Section 107 introduces the concept of fair dealing or as it is put there 'fair use' into American statutes for the first time. Fair use had been missing from the provisions of the 1909 Law, and the defence had been available through court decisions only. The purposes for which fair use may be a defence are such as 'criticism, comment, news reporting, teaching (including multiple copies for classroom use), scholarship or research.' The considerations that will help to decide any individual case are given in the law as four factors:

'(1) the purpose and character of the use, including whether such use is of a commercial nature or is for nonprofit educational purposes;

(2) the nature of the copyrighted work;

(3) the amount and substantiality of the portion used in relation to the copyrighted work as a whole; and

(4) the effect of the use upon the potential market for or value of the copyrighted work.'

The later Section 108(f)(4) states categorically that libraries may have the protection of this Section where appropriate. However, it would be hard to see how these factors could aid in deciding any individual case of possible infringement if there were not also a set of Guidelines dealing more closely with quantities of copied material. But these Guidelines do not form part of the text of the law, and may be varied at the instigation of the principals who have signed them. The Guidelines are discussed in more detail later (809-16).

Exceptions for libraries

807 Section 108 is headed 'Limitations on exclusive rights: reproduction by libraries and archives'. Broadly it allows for single copy copying for users on the following terms:

(1) the copy must be non-profit making, made by a library open to the public or at least to non-affiliated researchers, and there must be a notice of copyright on the copy

(2) in the case of unpublished works the right to copy applies only for preservation purposes or as a substitute for loan to another library also open to the public

(3)   a copy may be made to replace a damaged or lost copy, if the library has been unable to obtain a replacement at a fair price

(4)   in the case of a library requesting a copy, for one of its users, from another library, that copy may be made and supplied if it is a periodical article, a contribution to a collected work, or a small part of another work; but only if the copy becomes the property of the user and is for private study, scholarship or research, and provided the library requesting the copy carries a notice warning its users of copyright

(5)   complete or substantial parts of a work may be supplied to a user from a library's own collections if a copy cannot be obtained at a fair price, but only under the same conditions as (4) above

(6)   copyright liability will not fall on library staff for any infringement made by unsupervised use of copying equipment, provided a suitable notice is displayed, but persons using such equipment or making requests are fully liable for any infringement

(7)   a limited number of copies of an audiovisual news programme may be made and lent by a library

(8)   the privilege of fair use (Section 107) is also available to libraries

(9)   contractual obligations taken on by a library at the time of purchase are not affected by this Section

(10) although the same item may be copied more than once on isolated and unrelated occasions, libraries may not knowingly supply multiple copies either together or separately over a period of time, for 'aggregate use by one or more individuals or for separate use by the individual members of a group'

(11) 'systematic reproduction' of copies is not allowed by this Section, but the provision of copies through inter-library arrangements is allowed, provided they do not result in a requesting library receiving so many copies from a work that they aggregate into a substitute for a subscription to that work (if a periodical) or a purchase (if another kind). These inter-library arrangements are the subject of the third set of Guidelines, considered later (813)

(12) all these rights for library and archives reproduction apply to any category of material protected by copyright under (2) or (3) above — that is preservation or loan for research to another library, or to replace missing or damaged copies

(13) these rights do not otherwise apply to musical works, pictorial, graphic or sculptural works, to motion pictures or other audiovisual works, other than news programmes. Pictorial or graphic works may be copied when accompanying authorised extracts or parts of works

(14) this Section will be reviewed after every five years, by the Register of Copyrights, after consultations with owners and users representatives, to see how well it is meeting the aim of balancing the rights of the one with the needs of the other.

Perhaps the single most unexpected aspect of these library exceptions is that they all apply equally to gramophone records ('phonorecords') as to printed matter.

Differences from British law

808   Some other points of difference between the US law and British law may be noted:

(1)   there is no obligation on the maker of the copy to charge the recipient for it

(2) the criterion of 'public' libraries is wider than in the UK, allowing industrial or commercial libraries to participate if they are open to 'other persons doing research in a specialised field'

(3) copying between libraries of complete or substantial works or for users depends, essentially, on the work being unobtainable at a fair price, and not on obtaining permission from or being unable to trace the copyright owner

(4) extracts complete in themselves, 'contributions to a copyrighted collection' may be copied and are not regarded as a substantial part — this would apply to conference proceedings and symposia, contributed chapters, etc.

(5) liability will not fall on library employees who observe the rules: they cannot be sued for acts of infringement on their machines of which they are unaware

(6) the fair use defence may be used for certain copying acts beyond these limits

(7) these conditions can be over-ridden by contractual agreements between libraries and vendors of the materials they purchase: in other words publishers can opt out of the libraries exceptions

(8) musical works in copyright are not treated as other printed matter, and it would not be permitted under Section 108 to copy extracts for libraries or users, even were a piece of music to form a periodical article.

Guidelines

809 Next we consider the Guidelines provided for interpreting parts of the law. These are not part of the law, but are compiled for and accepted by the House [of Representatives] Judiciary Committee. There are three sets of Guidelines: two for Section 107 on educational copying from books and periodicals, and educational users of music; and one for Section 108 on library reproduction. They are prefaced by warnings that not only do they hold no legal force, but they are liable to amendment, nor are they to limit the types of copying under fair use (Section 107) or 'determinative in themselves or with respect to other situations' (Section 108).

Educational copying and guidelines

810 Guidelines on Educational Copying from Books and Periodicals states that copies may be made as follows:

(1) by or for a teacher in single copies for research or class use; a chapter from a book, an article from a periodical or newspaper, short story, essay or poem, whether from a collective work or not, and a chart, graph, diagram, drawing, cartoon or picture

(2) multiple copies for classroom may be made if they meet certain conditions:
   (a) brevity and spontaneity (defined below)
   (b) the cumulative effect test (defined below)
   (c) include a notice of copyright

(3) copying is not allowed if it:
   (a) replaces or substitutes for anthologies, e.g. by an accumulation of short extracts from various works
   (b) is from 'consumables' such as workbooks, test booklets, etc.

(c) substitutes for purchases, or is directed by a teacher's superior, or the same item is repeated from term to term
(d) is charged for to the pupil beyond the cost of making the copy.

811 The definitions of brevity, spontaneity and cumulative effect for multiple copying provide the following quantities and conditions:

Brevity

(1) a poem of less than 250 words or printed on not more than two pages, or an excerpt from a longer poem of not more than 250 words
(2) a complete prose item of less than 2500 words, an excerpt of 1000 words, or 10% of the complete work whichever is the less, down to a minimum of 500 words
(3) one illustrative item per book or periodical issue
(4) certain 'special' works of less than 2500 words combining language with illustrations may not be copied completely, but any excerpt of not more than two pages or 10% of the words may be.

Spontaneity

(5) copying must be at the instigation of the individual teacher
(6) the time between the decision to use the work and its use is too short to allow permission to be sought

Cumulative effect

(7) only one course in a school may use the copies
(8) only one complete work or two extracts from the same author may be made in one term, or not more than three items from the same periodical or collective work
(9) any one course may have no more than nine instances of such copying in a term.

Music — educational copying guidelines

812 Guidelines for Educational Uses of Music envisage the following uses:

(1) emergency copying for imminent performances, provided purchased copies are substituted later
(2) excerpts of performable units, for study, provided they are not more than 10% of the whole. Copies not to exceed one per pupil
(3) printed copies may be edited or simplified provided no distortion results, but words may not be altered or added
(4) a single recording of a student performance may be made and retained for study purposes
(5) single copy sound recordings may be made from recordings possessed by the school or teacher for the purpose of constructing aural exercises or examinations (this exemption applies only to musical copyright, not to copyright in the recording).

Library reproduction guidelines

813 Guidelines for Library Reproduction were prepared by CONTU and submitted to the House Judiciary Committee as suitable for inclusion in the House Conference Report. They refer to Section 108(g)(2) and interpret the law with regard to inter-library arrangements. Their main purpose is to define the 'aggregate quantities' of copy supply that would effectively substitute for a subscription to a periodical or purchase of a book.

814 In the case of periodicals the Guidelines say that six or more copies of an article or articles published in the same periodical within a period of five years prior to the request, and asked for within a calendar year, would substitute for a subscription. Items published earlier than five years before the date of request are not taken into account. In the case of books etc., six or more copies (including recordings) from a work within a year by one requesting entity is deemed to be a substitution for purchase. This will apply to the whole period the work is in copyright.

815 In both cases, if the requesting library has a subscription in force or on order, or a copy of the other item in stock or on order, then requests for copies of it are not counted as though contributing towards the six or more copies that would substitute a subscription.

816 Libraries not entitled to make copies under other parts of Section 108 are not allowed to make requests of other libraries under these guidelines for 108(g)(2). Requesting libraries must accompany requests with a statement that it is made in conformity with the Guidelines, and they must maintain records of all requests for copies they make that are covered by the Guidelines, and keep such records at least three years after the end of the year the request was made. The Guidelines themselves are to be reviewed five years after the bill (i.e. the Copyright Law) comes into force, i.e. 1st January 1983.

Warning of copyright notice

817 In November 1977 the final text of the Warning of copyright notice was issued. This warning is for use at places where libraries and archives accept requests for copies and on forms used by libraries for requesting copies (including records). The text is as follows:

> 'Notice
> 'Warning concerning copyright restrictions
> 'The copyright law of the United States (Title 17, United States Code) governs the making of photocopies or other reproductions of copyright material.
> 'Under certain conditions specified in the law, libraries and archives are authorized to furnish a photocopy or other reproduction, One of these specified conditions is that the photocopy or reproduction is not to be "used for any purpose other than private study, scholarship or research". If a user makes a request for, or later uses, a photocopy or reproduction for purposes in excess of "fair use", that user may be liable for copyright infringement.
> 'This institution reserves the right to refuse to accept a copying order if, in its judgement, fulfilment of the order would involve violation of copyright law.'

Interpretations

818 American commentators on the new law have already found some difficulties of interpretation. The interplay of fair use (Section 107) and library exceptions (Section 108) gives varying degrees of freedom, but this is not causing too much of a problem, since libraries may operate under either protection, provided they meet the requirements of not-for-profit operation. This definition is still confused, since contradictory Congressional rulings have been issued. The first said that copying in a commercial undertaking's library would not be admissible under Section 108, the second that it would, provided the copy itself was not made for profit; 'the "advantage"', said this later report, 'must attach to the immediate commercial motivation behind the reproduction or distribution itself, rather than to the ultimate profit-making motivation behind the enterprise in which the library is located.' It was just such an argument that was lost in the case of the British 1956 Act and its regulations (see 241-2). Beyond this hurdle, before the library in a for-profit organisation could use Section 108, it would have to interpret whether the purpose of its copying was covered by the phrase 'private study, scholarship or research', which effectively means, does the word 'private' govern research as well as study?

819 Cases of permitted copying and contractual agreements conflicting are more likely to arise with leased or borrowed items or with unpublished materials than with normally purchased publications, but it is possible for such restrictions to be imposed at point of sale and upheld over the authority of Section 108. In any case unpublished works may be copied under Section 108 only by the library or archives of which they form part of the current collection. A further condition is that copying must be in facsimile form (i.e. not a reading on record, etc.). The problem of unpublished items being at risk has been raised in the light of the Whitford Report's recommendation for an end to perpetual copyright (see 537).

820 An interesting variant on the declaration for private study etc. required to be obtained by British libraries under the Regulations, is that the US law speaks of a library having had no notice that a copy is to be used for any other purpose.This must stem from the intention of the law not to make librarians responsible for the infringements of others.

Systematic reproduction

821 One earlier cause for concern in the American library world was the wording 'systematic reproduction' as one of the acts prohibited in Section 108. Some thought this would preclude a library having a system for handling requests; but the wording of 108(g)(2) makes it clear enough to the layman's eye that 'systematic reproduction' refers to bulk copying sufficient to substitute for subscription or purchase. However, the phrase is not actually defined. A fine point about the exclusion of articles more than five years old from the 'rule of five' calculation as it might be called is that the Guidelines do not say they have no bearing on whether a subscription is being substituted, but imply that a calculation on their effect is perhaps to be worked out some time in the future. Thus one cannot say that 10 copies of articles made from issues of a periodical five to ten years old are suppliable to a requesting library as within the Guidelines. One presumably has to rely for a defence to this action on fair use under Section 107.

Supplying libraries

822 A very important point still in doubt concerns the copying operations of the supplying libraries. Since the receiving or requesting library is the one that has to satisfy the conditions, it appears that the supplying library must be legally in the clear. However, the scale of operation of the supplying library was certainly in the minds of CONTU when they prefixed the Guidelines with a remark about organisations that 'exist for the specific purpose of providing a central source for photocopies. Of course, these guidelines would not apply to such a situation'. So no National Library of Medicine-scale operations; and no BLLD? It is noted that copies regarded as infringing may not be imported. A library in a non-profit organisation is unable to shelter under Section 108 for its liability for infringement if it installs an unsupervised copier for its own staff.

823 Thus already the US law is beginning to get fuddled with conflicting opinions. One of the reasons is unclear language in the text of the law itself. To elucidate this, commentators go back to the Senate Judiciary Committee which was followed by the Senate-House Conference. The reports of these deliberations sometimes offer conflicting opinions, and they relate to different states of the text. To elucidate the law we also have Guidelines that are not statutory, but are endorsed by legislative bodies, and we even have explanatory notes on how to interpret the Guidelines. If there is a lesson for British librarians, publishers and legislators in all this, it must be: don't do it this way.

Problems remaining

824 But the total package is a comprehensive attempt to get a practical solution to the problem of what is just for both parties, and its detail deserves our close attention. The Whitford Committee did not venture into such choppy waters. The American experience with the working of this law will certainly be watched with close interest. After one year of operation we learn that although problem areas were indeed developing, there was general satisfaction with the overall provisions.

The problems concerned fairly small points of interpretation that led to copyright owners and users taking opposite viewpoints. Some of these were:

(1)   whether libraries were in fact free to use the 'fair use' provisions of Section 107 to *exceed* what was allowed under Section 108
(2)   can cassettes be recorded for circulation purposes from discs, if cassettes are not available?
(3)   can libraries handle photocopies given them by others? .
(4)   how does one define isolated and unrelated copying?
(5)   how many periodical articles can one copy for interloan that are over five years old?
(6)   when does a library become a system?
(7)   how far can for-profit organisations' libraries use Section 108?

Further developments

825   There has also been a debate on off-the-air video-taping, and a suit has been brought, but under the 1909 law. CONTU's final report recommended only one change in the new law, to take account of commercial copiers, and was generally of the opinion that the law should be given a fair run before any major changes were proposed. The Register of Copyrights, in the Library of Congress, now has an advisory committee which has already tabled a number of recommendations mostly giving the Copyright Office more work to do in fact finding.

Copy clearance and supply

826   The Copyright Clearance Center, Inc., was formed in 1977 as a non-profit corporation to provide publishers' permissions for journal article copying and to collect fees for the permissions. This would be for copying beyond fair use and Section 108 Guidelines. 2100 journals were reported to have registered with CCC, at fees ranging from $0.20 to $7.50 per page. While some libraries, including Library of Congress, have joined, CCC has had only a limited success in its early stages. A further development is a National Periodicals Center (NPC) which plans to supply copies of articles to libraries and individuals, and to collect agreed copyright fees. NPC is to be part of the Library of Congress. Yet another facility was being offered by the National Technical Information Service (NTIS). Primarily established to distribute the results of government funded research and development, via the AD and PB series of reports, the NTIS has interpreted its brief more widely and has established a photocopy service for periodical articles, based not on a central collection, but on agencies such as BLLD. NTIS will serve only regular customers, numbered at about 12,000. Publishers signed up for this service were being offered a 50 cent royalty for each article copied, without regard to the length of the article.

Australia

827   In the same month as the US Copyright Law's enactment, some four
       or five months before our own Copyright Committee reported, the
       Australian Franki Committee submitted its report. The Committee,
       consisting of four lawyers, had been set up in June 1974 to examine
       the problem of facsimile reproduction and to advise on any necessary
       change in the Australian copyright law. The 'Franki Report' (ref. 151)
       deals then with a small part of the whole copyright area. One of the
       spurs to set up the enquiry was probably the widely publicised case
       of University of New South Wales v. Moorhouse and another; as a
       result of which the University was held responsible for allowing a
       breach of copyright to occur on one of its self-service copiers. The
       circumstance that the machine had no warning notice about copyright
       lessened the value of this would-be test case.

828   The Franki Report is a positively Australian production, and reflects
       Australia's position as a large and developed country, yet with a small
       population scattered over vast distances and with few large centres of
       industry or learning; a position which has led to great reliance on
       publications from overseas. The Report also reflects the geographical
       isolation of the country and its mental allegiances divided between the
       traditions and practice of the United States and Britain.

829   The Australian Copyright Act of 1968-73 is based firmly on the
       British of 1956, but with some significant differences. As far as fair
       dealing goes the provisions are similar to the 1956 Act — equally
       undefined — but in the special provision for libraries (Sections 48-51),
       persons receiving copies made by libraries (not-for-profit is specified)
       must satisfy the librarians that they will be used only for research or
       private study. This compares with the statutory declaration required
       by the 1956 Act. More importantly, a copy of a reasonable part of a
       work other than a periodical article may be supplied without any
       further requirement (the 1956 Act requires copyright clearance by
       reasonable enquiry). But, as in the British Act, the whole of a work
       or more than a reasonable part may be copied for another library under
       Australian law provided the librarian does not know and could not by
       reasonable enquiry discover the name of the copyright owner. Where
       unpublished works are in libraries open to public inspection, copies
       may be made for research or private study or with a view to publica-
       tion, 50 years after the death of the author and 75 years after the
       workk was completed. In the 1956 Act the periods are 50 and 100
       years. The Australian Act also provides for theses or similar literary
       works to be copied by university or similar libraries, for users who
       satisfy the librarian they are wanted for research or private study.

Franki Report recommendations

830 The Franki Committee recommend modifying the 1968-73 Act's provisions in the following ways (among others):

(1) the words 'research or private study' should throughout be amended to 'research or study', and half of the committee consider any personal use should be permitted in such contexts

(2) the Act be amended to remove librarians' liability for infringing use of self-service copying machines, provided a warning notice is displayed

(3) fair dealing should be qualified for reprographic reproduction purposes: these should be considerations used:
   (a) purpose and character of the dealing
   (b) nature of the work
   (c) the amount and substantiality of the portion taken in relation to the whole work
   (d) whether the work can be obtained within a reasonable time at a normal commercial price
   (e) the effect of the dealing upon the potential market for or value of the work

(4) fair dealing should allow the copying of a single periodical article, or more than one where the subject matter is the same; and in other works copying not more than one chapter or 10% whichever is the greater

(5) 'reasonable portion' should be defined as one chapter or 10% of a work

(6) copying by a library for a user of a complete work or more than a reasonable portion be allowed where the librarian is unable to obtain an unused copy at a normal commercial price, and makes a declaration to this effect

(7) payment for copies supplied by libraries be not required, and libraries be not permitted to make a profit from making copies

(8) the requirement that a librarian be satisfied about the purpose of a copy be replaced by a declaration from the user about the proposed use (for research or study, or other phrase)

(9) copying for other libraries be permitted without the proviso that the receiving library declare no other copy to have been received, apart from lost, destroyed or damaged copies

(10) declarations from users of copies, supplied from one library to another, should also contain a signed declaration about their purpose

(11) the recommendation in (9) above should not apply where libraries require copies for their own shelves

(12) copying between libraries be permitted as recommended in (6) above

(13) unpublished works in libraries be permitted to be copied for preservation, security, research, in the original or another library, provided this does not cause them to be published

(14) damaged, deteriorating, lost or stolen copies can be replaced by copies, provided unused copies cannot be obtained at a normal commercial price

(15) microfilm or microfiche copies be allowed where the original is to be destroyed.

831 Other recommendations of interest apply to multiple copying for non-profit educational use:

(1) institutions be permitted to make up to six copies of a periodical

article, provided they are used in the library and eventually destroyed

(2) up to six copies of a work or a substantial part may be made provided copies cannot be obtained at a normal commercial price, provided they are used in the library and eventually destroyed

(3) a statutory licence scheme be introduced for multiple copies for classroom use, to incorporate recording what copies are made and an obligation to pay a royalty if demanded within, say, three years

(4) such a scheme should cover a limited amount of copying, such as the whole of a work not separately published; the whole of a work of which copies cannot be obtained at a normal commercial price; one article, or more than one if on the same subject matter; not more than a reasonable portion (to be defined as 10% or one chapter of a work, whichever is greater)

(5) such a scheme should exclude as free copying any instances of copying up to two pages or 1% (whichever is greater) of a work or of two or more works in multiple copies, once in any period of 14 days

(6) teachers be permitted to make up to three copies of a work or part of a work for classroom use, under the statutory licensing scheme

(7) correspondence educational institutions be permitted to copy for students, copies up to the amount permitted to be copied by libraries for users, but without requiring requests from students.

832   These provisions are quite generous in the context of the detailed provisions laid down in the American copyright law — multiples are more readily permitted to education, and there are no restrictions on cumulative effect on copying between libraries. The phrase that keeps cropping up in the recommendations, 'normal commercial price', may lead to some disputes, since Australia has now no retail price maintenance for books, and what looks exorbitant in one place may be normal in another. With these three words are others we have omitted in the summarised recommendations: 'within a reasonable time'. It must be remembered that about 90% of typical library materials in Australia are imported, and it would be unreasonable to require libraries to delay copying for several months while waiting for ordered books to arrive. This shortage of internally produced literature may have contributed to the overall impression given by the Franki Report that the user is by far the more important of the two parties to be considered. 'Little comfort for publishers in the Franki Report' ran the *Bookseller* headline. Certainly there is no sense of publishing being at risk through reprographic copying. 'If the publication of a journal is for a commercial purpose', they say, 'the publisher must be prepared to meet the changes in technology and in the habits of the community.' They do not appear to have thought that one way the commercial problems may be met is by modifying the law.

European Economic Community

833   Many countries are examining their copyright laws and a study of all available information on recent changes and proposals would no doubt

be thought-provoking in the context of this study. But within the limits of a short account of present practice and future prospects for copyright law of interest to librarians in the United Kingdom, it would be unrealistic to go very much further. This chapter is therefore concluded with a cursory summary of the position in the EEC countries, restricting the angle to photocopying, as set out in Adolf Dietz' study (ref. 140), of which the English translation was published in 1978, from a German original of the previous year.

Dietz : Copyright law in the European Community

834   There are those who would say Dietz' approach is tendentious from the start. The relevant chapter is headed 'Claims to compensation for unverifiable mass untilization of works (sound and video recording; photocopying),' and he takes it for granted that 'the authors and their legal successors cannot remain unprotected in this field and must at least have a claim to fair compensation, since otherwise the primary production of the basic printed document might cease as it would no longer pay.' He regards the current general use of photocopies in the EEC as an 'infringement of Article 9 Para 2 of the RBC [revised Berne Convention] under which normal exploitation of the work may not be prejudiced by exceptions to the copyright protection.' This infringement he finds 'taken for granted in all countries.'

Belgium and Luxembourg

835   In Belgium and Luxembourg there is no legislation for exceptions by photocopying to copyright protection. This means that every time a copy is made without permission the law is broken. Remedies proposed, in Belgium at least, have generally tried to establish contractual arrangements rather than modify the law.

France

836   In France the making of copies is restricted to private use, though a recent case involving the Centre National de Recherche Scientifique has confused the issue to the extent of making it appear that collective use may be permitted if it is for the purposes of research. One solution to the problem has been the introduction, outside copyright law, of a tax on the sale of most books (school books and scientific works are among those excepted), and on the sale of reprography equipment. The proceeds go not to individual writers or publishers but for the general improvement of writing and books, to a Centre National des Lettres. The former 'domaine public payant' has been discontinued. Dietz' comment is that although this solution is outside copyright law, it is of the type that could be embodied in copyright regulations. At present the French measure is criticised since it is unrelated to the extent of copying, and may appear to give *carte blanche* to any copying practice.

Italy

837 In Italy, photocopies are permissible if made in libraries for personal use or for the library service. No recompense is offered. Proposals to curb the flow of copying that has resulted have looked to collective agreements between the users and copyright owners.

Germany

838 The Federal Republic of Germany, with a recent (1965) copyright act has gone further than most countries towards recognising the rights of copyright owners. While the law introduced a levy on equipment for sound and video recorders, the extent of photocopying for private use did not warrant a similar levy on the sale of photocopiers. Instead, there is provision for a claim to compensation for copying for commercial purposes. This commercial purpose copying, more limited than that for private use, allows only small parts of works or single articles to be copied, but up to seven copies may, it is thought, be allowed to be made. Non-commercial copying but not privately done, is also allowed on this scale, and without fees being levied. Thus copying, by education, public bodies and libraries is freely allowed. Dietz reckons that while the limits of copying are fairly clear, the German law makes too little allowance for encroachments on normal exploitation. The compensation paid for use (by an arrangement between the Federal Association of German Industry and the collecting agency, known as VG Wissenschaft) was reported in 1976 to be less than $\frac{1}{2}$ million Deutschmarks, which Dietz says bears no relation to the amount of copying done in industry. (See ref. 147 for later developments.)

Denmark

839 In Denmark there is a special provision for copies made by libraries and archives. By this single copies of articles and short extracts may be made. Copies may also be made for 'private use' by firms and other corporate bodies. No payments are made to copyright owners for this privilege, but there were in 1974 proposals to amend the law, at the same time restricting the amount of free copying, and extending the scope of copying, by schools, etc., that should attract payments.

United Kingdom

840 The account of the United Kingdom arrangements will be omitted here, as it has been covered in chapter 1, though it is worth noting Dietz' comments on the BLLD's service. The fact that 500 customers are overseas, and that the service includes copies from foreign literature, shows there is a 'European dimension' to this copyright problem. This all makes the need for a solution to the problem more urgent, he says. The Irish situation is mentioned briefly, and Dietz merely notes that there are no regulations for libraries in the Irish law, a rare example of that law differing from the British.

Netherlands

841   The Netherlands arrangements are dealt with last, because, Dietz says, they are very recent and the most detailed attempt to sort out the problems caused by photocopying. Similar to the German law, the Dutch law (1974) also allows free private copying, but allows corporate use (in public bodies, schools, etc.) only in return for compensation. Unlike the German law, there is a limit on the quantity that may be copied for personal private use — only short articles and small parts of works.

842   Institutions are differentiated in what they may copy, divided into public administration, libraries, education and other bodies acting in the public interest. For example, fees paid by libraries are 10 Dutch cents per page, while only $2\frac{1}{2}$ Dutch cents are charged for school copying. Although no specific method for collecting the fees is set out in the law, a collecting society 'Reprorecht' has been formed. Other organisations not included in the four categories specified above may, for a fee, copy from academic works only, and distribute to employees only. Dietz feels that despite these comprehensive arrangements, the Dutch law is still unsatisfactory as it allows free copying for strictly private use, and there is an increasing number, he says, of miniature copiers in the private sector.

843   However, in assessing prospects for a harmonisation of the nine countries' copyright laws in the field of photocopying, Dietz favours a modification of the Dutch method, as it is the one to come closest to accommodating in the owners' interest the actual copying practices observed in all countries.

Documentation centres

844   Finally Dietz introduces the subject of making copies from copies, i.e. using microforms as masters for further reproduction or storing data automatically, practices characteristic of documentation centres. Apart from observing that the copying act must be reckoned to occur in the input of the item to the store, a natural enough assumption, he then shies away from further discussion as 'discussion on this matter is still too much in a state of flux.' In his defence it must be said that Dietz' brief was to compare the nine countries' laws, and in this area, apart from a provision in the Dutch law, there is nothing to compare.

Harmonization prospects

845   Summing up, Dietz rejects as models for a harmonized system the

negative approach of France, Belgium and Luxembourg in which although free copying is not permitted yet there is no machinery for copyright owners to gain fair reward from use of their materials. He also rejects the method of the UK, Denmark and Italy, in which the exceptions to copyright cover too large a sector (including libraries). The German and Dutch systems point in the right direction, but need stricter limits on free copying. Because of 'the non-existent or unsatisfactory arrangements in most countries, this is an area which is particularly well-suited for harmonization or unification on a European scale.'

Euronet

846 A certain urgency has been brought to the EEC consideration of copyright since Dietz' report by the needs of Euronet. This computer network of data banks and data bases, input by a multitude of 'host' organisations, with centres of access in all nine EEC countries, consists predominantly of abstracts and indexes of bibliographical items — journal articles and reports in the main. The heavily increased awareness of (principally) scientific literature this system is expected to bring about was thought by its organisers to be likely to increase the demand for access to the document, and to be likely to endanger the balance of publishing economics if a solution was not found that made financial allowance for publishers' interests. (Librarians on the other hand are sceptical, feeling that document awareness is already high, and they put greater emphasis on the role of availability in increasing demand, and believe that in any case document supply has little to do with financial viability of journal publishing. This they associate more with the general economic climate, and the resources given to libraries to purchase the materials they need.)

Franklin Institute Report

847 Since there is no quite comparable equivalent of the British Library Lending Division in the other eight countries, an early question that arose concerned the means available to users of Euronet for obtaining copies of the articles and reports to which they would be referred. An investigation of the problems of setting up a 'document delivery' system was therefore carried out by the Franklin Institute GmbH, of Munich. This went into considerable detail on the legal obstacles in the nine countries placed by the existence of copyright law. Three ways of presenting the Euronet user with his document were considered, and two of them — photocopy and devices for non-material text transmission, or facsimile transmission — were thought to pose copyright problems. Paul D. Gillespie and his co-authors in the Report (ref. 143) find that a BLLD-type operation of photocopy supply would be legal only in Denmark and the Netherlands, apart from the

U.K., but even in the U.K., the requirement for declarations as to the use to which photocopies are being put would pose difficulties.

848   After a fairly lengthy discussion of the different difficulties in the nine countries (for example, making the copy is frequently only half of the problem: distributing it has sometimes different restrictions), the report concludes that 'negotiation of licence agreements with the copyright owners seems to be the most advisable permanent solution of the Euronet document delivery problem.' They point to the NTIS in the U.S. as providing a workable solution with its JACS (Journal Article Copying Service), based on formal agreements with publishers. The Institute of Scientific Information's OATS (Original Article Tear Sheet) service is also mentioned as a good interim model to follow while a more formal NTIS-type agency is set up. I.S.I. supply either original text pages from surplus copies, or photocopies when these are exhausted. A self-imposed fee (70 cents per article is reported) is paid by I.S.I. to the publisher, financed from the $3.50 charged to the requester of the article.

849   The Franklin Institute report concludes with a recommendation that a system be initiated by contacting copyright owners via the appropriate international associations, with a proposal that a fee paying service (DM1 or DM2 is mentioned as a reasonable sum to pay per item) be negotiated. Only journal articles, it is suggested, would be appropriate for inclusion in such a scheme.

Document Delivery Workshop

850   The Franklin Institute report appeared in 1978, and in November 1979, an EEC Workshop on Document Delivery was held in Luxembourg. No positive progress, however, was made, because of the opposed viewpoints of publishing and library interests. It would seem, after the event, that the Workshop was an ill-judged attempt by EEC to begin harmonisation of European national copyright law by imposing conditions for document supply on several member countries whose law did not require any changes for them to continue to supply documents in the context of Euronet. As far as the U.K. was concerned, it seems possible that EEC officials assumed that the Whitford Committee's recommendations on reprography were virtually certain of general acceptance.

9
Discussion and Outlook

901 The last chapter may not seem a suitable place to begin discussing the nature and theory of a subject, but that is what I feel needs to be done here. I have tried to explain how the British copyright law moved to its present state, how it can be interpreted by librarians, and something of current proposals for change, and for purposes of comparison what is happening in a few other countries. But I have largely omitted talking about the basic purpose of copyright. To offer a reasoned argument about not what is likely to happen, but what by rights should happen, it is essential to go into such fundamentals.

902 Copyright is not a simple concept. Compared, say, with the right to free speech it offers far greater complexity. It has at its root a duality of purpose that can be seen in its first shape as a monopoly of printing granted by the State to the Stationers' Company in exchange for the opportunity of censoring undesirable material. The first modern legal provision, though, the Act of 1709, shows the still basically two-sided nature of copyright, in its title: 'An Act for the encouragement of learning by vesting the "Copies" of printed books in the authors or purchasers of such copies during the times herein mentioned.' The Preamble reinforces this idea by stating the purpose of the Act as 'for preventing such [piratical] practice and for the encouragement of learned men to compose and write useful books.' Thus the notion of affording protection to authors, a limited monopoly, for the general benefit of learning, in the public interest.

903 So copyright is not an absolute right, and it is not a form of property. If other things are for the encouragement of learning, one begins to see, they may prevail against copyright. Copyright is more in the nature of a bargain struck between state and author, and like many bargains it has been negotiated over the years on different terms, taking the form of the various statutes. The late Verner Clapp, a doughty fighter for library interests, could only see the process as a dwindling of the freedom of libraries and others, representing the public interest. Speaking in the context of American law in 1970, (ref. 119) he would have seen his remarks as equally applicable to this country:

> 'The copyright industry has been pretty successful. It has succeeded in doubling the period both of the original and renewal term [Queen Anne's Act protected for 14 years plus another 14; the US 1909 Act for 28 years renewable for another 28] . . . In addition, copyright, which consisted originally merely in the monopoly of printing the copyrighted work, has since been extended to include rights of performance, translation, condensation and adaptation.'

Clapp sees the story as one of progressive erosion of the rights of purchasers of a work:

> 'For example, he may not read it aloud for profit if it is a story or poem, nor deliver it for profit if it is a lecture, sermon or address. He may not translate it, abridge it or adapt it. If it is a dramatic work he may not perform it publicly even if it is not for profit, and this prohibition runs to dramatic motion pictures and literary and musical compositions as well as to plays per se. He may still exhibit, lend, sell, give away, throw it at his wife or burn it. Although he may still copy from it for purposes of study, or permit another to do so his rights in this connection are badly clouded.'

904   I have given this much from Clapp's vivid paper to illustrate the fervour with which some espouse the rights of the public interest, and the sense of restriction they feel at the copyright owner's progress in securing an interest in the various forms of exploitation that are still ramifying to this day. But the other side of the argument is also fervid, and needs to be heard. R. F. Whale, (ref. 18) calls copyright a grave misnomer, having only partly to do with making copies and copying, and reminds us that in other languages it has a different name, 'droit d'auteur', 'derecho de autor', 'diritto d'autore', and 'Urheberecht'. After the Act of 1709 there was still, he says, a common law right in literary property apart from that conferred by copyright, and assignable under it, and that common law right belonged to the author. This was eventually abolished in 1911. The idea behind the common law right was, to quote Whale, that

> 'the creative act established between the author and his work rights of a moral or personal nature, but these rights, if they existed, were not comprehended within the statute, which envisaged only the more limited purpose of regulating the book trade.'

905   This attitude to copyright as incorporating moral as well as commercial rights is reflected in the 1971 text of the Berne Convention, which the UK will have to decide on. The Whitford Report recommends suitable amendments to the law to accommodate moral rights of authors, but is doubtful how far the necessary protection is lacking: the law of passing off, and the Trades Descriptions Act may already give sufficient protection. Elsewhere in their Report, the Whitford Committee seem to concentrate on the act of copying as being the crucial factor in deciding on whether new situations and technology present potential

infringements, as for example in the case of computers. The fact that the law already covers performance as a restricted act, makes it strange that the Committee did not look at the concept of use as its criterion rather than copying. One notes, too, that translation, adaptation, etc., are not simple acts of physical copying.

Public Lending Right

906 At this point it is time to consider the place of Public Lending Right. Although the idea of including public lending as one of the acts restricted by copyright was not proceeded with, and PLR eventually scrambled onto the statute book unconnected with copyright, it does seem logical to regard it as closely related. Similarly performers' protection rights are not part of the copyright legislation, but are treated as akin, and textbooks deal with them together. So one expects PLR to grow closer to copyright, and perhaps eventually be incorporated into it. When the possibility, or feasibility, rather, of extending PLR to works lent communally by other institutions than public libraries is brought to realisation, could well be the occasion. The fact that PLR was specifically excluded from the Whitford Committee's terms of reference supports the view that it is an intellectually related idea.

907 It is not my intention to go deeply into the justice of the case for PLR, but I must record my conviction that it is a logical and reasonable development of authors' protection. Whatever one may say about the influence of public lending on individual sales seems irrelevant in the context of copyright. For instance no-one claims the right to put on a public performance of an adaptation of a novel without paying a royalty to the author. One does not use the argument that such a performance doesn't detract from sales of the book, and may even increase them. Such an argument, even if established as true, would be irrelevant. The point is that usage of the author's work is exploitation of a literary property. Were the argument to be taken further, that profit taking was a crucial factor; that in the public library it is absent, in the theatrical performance it is present, and the 'public interest' is served by the non-profit service; then one can envisage a local authority-sponsored series of public performances of copyright works as a closer parallel. Again, one would not defend such communal use of a literary property as not warranting a royalty.

908 If the concept of public libraries infringing copyright, or authors' rights by lending books is still too difficult to swallow, one has to appeal to the factor of scale. It is certainly reasonable for a purchaser of a book to do all manner of acts with it in private — recite it, dramatise it, translate it for his own use if it should be in a language easier to read, and so on. When he brings other people into the scene, the question begins to get slightly distorted: one could imagine a private loan to a close friend; very well, then passing it round the members of a club he belongs to; buying a second copy so he can increase the circle of his borrowers, and so by gradual stages until he is advertising the free loan of copies to all and sundry, and is virtually running a public library. Very unlikely perhaps, as a process, but as a sequence of possible situations, it could be demonstrated. Somewhere along the line the act of lending has changed from private to public: a matter of degree, since the concepts involved are not precise.

909 I have gone into PLR thus far to draw the parallel with photocopying. The loan of a book to a reader from a public library will in due course attract a fee; the supply to a reader of a copy of an extract for his retention will not as yet bring in any reward to the author or publisher, even though the recipient pays for the copy. This situation does already occur in the Federal Republic of ermany, and it is acknowledged as anomalous. Certainly, for all those who accept the justice of PLR, the case for royalty payments for photocopies ought to be proven.

Investment and exploitation

910 Although in origin the copyright laws developed to protect the author from unjust exploitation and encourage him in his practice, and at the same time to afford the public the continued benefits of his work, the laws also protected the intermediaries, the publishers, from each other and from piracy of the works for which they were paying to distribute. This system works well enough when the means of distribution requires investment on a substantial scale; and breaks down if a large number of users can by-pass the official channel, i.e. the publisher. Still more problems arise when the author himself has little or no financial interest in his writings. His publisher is still committed to a heavy outlay, and though he is saved royalty payments, these rarely amount to as much as half his other expenses. It was for this reason that Section 15 of the Copyright Act was introduced to protect the publisher where there is no monopoly in the matter he is setting up in type.

Journals

911 When one comes to the learned journal scenario, the position of the publisher is hazardous in the extreme. The author has no financial interest in the prosperity of the publisher, but is concerned principally to disseminate his work: it is as often as not the direct result of his salaried or grant-aided employment. To further his end he will obtain offprints if he can to send out to his colleagues, and these will be supplied either free or at a modest 'run-on' cost above a certain number. He may even submit his article simultaneously to several journals, and allow two or more to publish unawares. At the other end of the communication system the journal is, admittedly, publicised

by being covered by indexing and abstracting journals. But though the sight of a new journal title in a secondary source for the first time must frequently lead to a subscription being placed, the featuring of a single article of interest is less likely to spur on a subscription to an established journal not held. Instead, libraries in all subject areas exist to serve the user with loans or photocopies of specific articles. Even the unclassified unannotated 'contents lists' media tend to focus their users' attention on single articles at a time rather than on the whole economic package of the journal subscription. As we have seen there is little or no evidence that all these facilities directly reduce subscriptions, but it must be admitted that the system is there that would enable libraries and individuals to economise if they have a mind to.

912　The typical scholarly or research journal is published by one of three kinds of body: the learned society, the university press or the commercial publisher. All need to cover their costs to survive, and preferably create a surplus. If the public interest were predominant in the dissemination pattern one would expect a subsidised publication produced by the bodies that fund the work. This seems not to happen very much; these bodies, governments or foundations, typically producing the primal report, unedited and unrefereed, when they produce anything at all. In view of the frequent outcry by users — especially librarians — when a journal publisher protests at a dissemination scenario that seems to be prejudicing his sales, and therefore his viability, it is strange that offers have not been made to take over this function into the public sector. Many journals are, for whatever reason, at a critically low level of subscription support, and one does not hear the reaction: we could do with a few less. New journals continue to appear — about 4% per annum — although some existing ones collapse, and one can only presume the same factor operates as with book publishing — one must keep numbers up to spread the load of the possible losses, and to give oneself the chance of the occasional jackpot.

913　The foregoing is a mere poke at the problem: it offers no solution to the continuance of serious journal publication, and is intended only to set the reader thinking. In the case of other publications there is a clearer picture in relation to copyright. As with journals there is the problem of fragmentation, though it is less acute. Tables from reference books, contributions from symposia, chapters from textbooks can all be in demand and all can be in danger from excessive photocopying. What the publisher has for sale is a package; one buys the reference book knowing of a need for one or two items in it, hoping to be able to justify the purchase by unpredicted future cumulative use. One knows of two or three valuable contributions in a symposium, and one buys the volume thinking that other pieces in it could be of interest too, perhaps later. In the same way a journal publisher expects that one takes a subscription to all his issues in the presumption that enough of them will arouse interest and sufficient satisfaction to continue the subscription another year. In other words, most publishers sell and most purchasers buy without the clear expectation of profitable use of everything in the purchase.

914   If one accepts this as a reasonable state of affairs, conducive to a wide variety of material being published allowing browsing, serendipity and other discursive and mind-broadening activities to take place, how can this be reconciled with the proposal that a publisher should make his book available for purchase in separate chapters, or journals in separate articles? The obvious reaction is that the economic basis of publishing would be changed completely. If people pay only for what they consciously need, the cost of producing each unit will increase dramatically: one might find the cost of a separate article in a journal carrying a hundred a year in normal publishing style, would amount to half the cost of a subscription. To buy at separate times four chapters of a twenty chapter book could exceed the cost of a copy of the complete work. Just as publishing is speculation on the part of the publisher, in that he does not know how many copies are certain to sell, so purchasing is speculation on the buyer's part, as he cannot tell whether the benefit received from it will justify, fall short of or exceed his outlay. While we have this multiplicity of outlet and of take up, the characteristics of diversity in publishing will remain. Take away the chance for viability of the new and untried product, reduce the publisher's gamble to money down the drain, and only the altruist will remain in business. It should be sufficiently obvious that I am pointing a finger at both the persistent journal article copier and the book's chapter divider, but let us look at a different setting where the same phenomenon is in danger of occurring: the secondary journal of index or abstract entries.

Abstracts and indexes

915   No-one begrudges abstracts journals their economic viability, and most accept that the heavy investment of staff time in preparing abstracts, classifying, indexing, printing and cumulating them is work well done and money well spent that the publisher is expected to recoup by spreading it over his subscription price. But each abstracts journal covers a wider range than most of its users will need. The largest journals, such as *Chemical Abstracts* and *Index Medicus* sell by virtue of their comprehensiveness to many customers interested in only a part of their subject matter. Competing journals in narrower subject areas frequently have less full coverage of the literature: so the large publications continue to be bought. But in recent years these same abstracts journals after a comparatively small scale activity in selling computer tapes of their publications, have been leasing them with much greater success to brokers who then offer an on-line information service. An on-line service can offer its users great advantages, especially in being able to search a cumulated data base in one operation instead of having to check numerous sequences, and the facility of combining search terms to produce a single result closer to one's need than a manual search can readily afford; and these advantages are of great appeal. To be able to search say, BNB from 1950-73 in one operation on BLAISE instead of through several printed cumulations, being able to fine down an *Index Medicus* search on MEDLINE by judiciously combining descriptions so as to produce the two or three items really relevant, are very attractive extras, and the success of on-line systems is at present reflecting that attraction.

916 But there is another side to the picture, which Dr. A. K. Kent has put more convincingly than I can (ref. 29). His view is that on-line systems are being provided at marginal costs at present: that is that their producers regard them as extra services to their conventional output (the printed data base as a set of abstracts or index entries), and price them only to give a return on the extra costs that computerisation involves. Kent's argument is that were the costs of constructing the data base to be properly shared out over on-line as well as print customers, the on-line service would be seen as very expensive. Further, the high cost of producing the data base may well lead to simplification in its coverage, as well as in its search strategies (since as Kent remarks, the most commercially successful service is a simple one). The parallel with the erosion of traditional print marketing is obvious. If libraries cancel their secondary source subscriptions in any numbers in order to pay for on-line services, they are in danger of losing the breadth of coverage they formerly had in the printed source. There is no difficulty over erosion of copyright in this instance, since by leasing contracts the owner keeps control of exploitation of his property. But the effect on the communication of ideas and knowledge, however, is likely to be damaging, just as in the cases where unfair usage of a publication, or the potential for unfair usage make it uneconomic to continue its publication.

Ideologies

917 We have now arrived, I think, at the point in the argument where ideologies come in. Should one back copyright to help save the small publisher and the minority author from being crowded out of the market? The tendency of government and large business combines to gain too large a proportion of the means of communication creates a danger of 'pushing' some information and withholding other. Newspapers are a crucial example of this. It could be that copyright would help to fight this tendency by safeguarding the rights of 'a plurality of information-sources . . . and retention in the "total information system" of a reasonably unconcentrated (i.e. not in too few hands) and undiversified commercial sector.' (ref. 153, p. 443). But though the Canadian author of this passage is proposing an argument for the retention of copyright, in his later remarks on libraries, he does not observe the centralizing influence that libraries also have, which when geared up into sophisticated co-operative systems and automated networks again threaten the viability of the very items their existence otherwise helps to preserve.

918   Solutions to copyright problems are never easy. I believe that the nature of the problem has not yet been seen by many of those who protest on one side about the author's, or publisher's dwindling rewards, an on the other about the encroachment of restrictions on the sensible exploitation of creative works for the good of all. The problem is simply one of scale. Just as it would be economic and helpful to take families out of houses and put them into flats, if it were not that the benefits they gain turn to outweighing disadvantages when the flats get too far from the ground, so with publications and their users. Not too many users can benefit from one copy of a periodical or book before the difficulties crowd in. So it is a question of maintaining the status quo, by counteracting the developments that threaten it; or of facing a new communications system.

Communications systems

919   What do we mean by a new communications system? The beginnings have been shown already: broadly it would be a transition from speculative to on-demand publishing: the synopsis journal with microfiche supplements of full texts of papers; or more probably, the list of contents with hard copy printout on demand. Even a strengthened refereeing system would in that context fail to stop a tendency towards authoritarianism, by removing the peer review and assessment that journals so valuably provide after publication. In the creative literature field one would find more and more reliance on material developed from radio and television, again published on demand, perhaps in expanded form. But again, the bottle neck of the media channels and the limited time they can give would tend to concentrate too much selection power in a few hands, and reduce the amount of easily accessible creation.

920   Being unable to see round the next corner any further than the next man, and being a gradualist by nature, I opt for the maintenance of a multiplicity of outlets for publications, by which as our Canadian economist puts it 'dissent and originality have a fighting chance of breaking through to the public, even when ulterior motives may be throttling or muffling them elsewhere'. (ref. 153, p. 443). This option leaves us, I believe, with three methods to choose from to keep the

balance between creators and users of copyright matrials. The fourth device, that of allowing natural market forces to solve the problem, being, as I have tried to show, ideologically unacceptable.

921 The three methods are restraint of co-operation between users, coupled perhaps with the charging of differential prices to organisations that engage in multiple use; subsidizing publication; and monitoring use and imposing a levy on that use, by whatever means seems best. Differentially higher prices to large users seems quite a reasonable means to employ: the H. W. Wilson indexes, for example, have been supplied on a service basis, related to the library's bookfunds. It is harder to see the possibility of restraint of co-operation. The best way to deter libraries from over-reliance on networks and borrowing agencies is to give them more money for purchases. Most libraries, as has been shown, will buy rather than borrow. Were funds to be restored to anything like their real purchasing power of the late sixties, both in the U.K. and America, there would be fewer complaints on both sides. Present day political tendencies however are so much against this level of public expenditure, probably because of world trade recessions or fears of recessions, that it seems idle to press the case. Subsidy of publication, also a government role if it were adopted, is unlikely to be more than highly selective, and should be discarded as a thoroughgoing solution for the same reasons.

922 The introduction of levies on usage (copying and lending alike) seems the fairest of solutions. It recognises actual use and therefore gives its rewards fairly. The method has been adopted piecemeal in West Germany, is being tentatively introduced in the United States, and is proposed for the United Kingdom. All that is required is a more overt recognition that use must be paid for, that library purchases are public exploitation of private investment and that exploitation must be paid for pro rata, and that public money must be found — whether through public libraries, schools, universities, colleges, or national institutions — if our present pattern of publication, which I for one believe to be valuable, though not perfect, is to be preserved.

Appendix 1

Copying and copyright

Are you within the law ?

Schools, colleges, libraries and institutions today use all kinds of copying machines. Much of the copying done is of non-copyright material and is unrestricted, but publishers are often asked about copyright and copying. Here are the essential facts:

Copyright is designed to protect the livelihood of the creators and producers of literary, dramatic, artistic and musical works.

Copyright lasts for 50 years from the death of the author or composer (or 50 years from posthumous publication).

Copyright also covers illustrations in books.

The typography of books published since September 1957 is also copyright for 25 years from publication, irrespective of whether the text or music is copyright.

Single copies of copyright material may be made for private study, provided no more than a 'reasonable proportion' is copied. The Society of Authors and the Publishers Association interpret this as follows:

A single extract of up to 4,000 words,
or
a series of extracts (none over 3,000 words) totalling up to 8,000 words
} but neither of these may exceed 10% of the whole work.

But poems, essays and other short works are treated as complete works — so permission is needed to copy these, or any musical works.

Multiple copies (e.g. class sets) **of copyright material** may **not** be made without prior permission
} permission to copy must be obtained and payment may have to be made.

If in doubt you should ask the publisher of the work.

For fuller details, see *Photocopying and the law*, available for 40p prepaid from The Publishers Association, 19 Bedford Square, London, WC1.

Please remember that the publisher is always willing to offer help and advice.

B C C British Copyright Council
in co-operation with
Publishers Association, Educational Publishers Council,
Music Publishers Association, Society of Authors.

---

reproduced by kind permission of the British Copyright Council. The Council wish to make clear that this poster was produced for schools and other educational institutions rather than libraries, and it consequently carries no mention of the Libraries Regulations.

Appendix 2

Addresses

Aslib, 3 Belgrave Square, London SW1X 8PL. Tel: 01-235 5050

Association of Learned and Professional Society Publishers, c/o 1 Birdcage Walk, London SW1H 9JJ

Authors Lending and Copyright Society Ltd, c/o Davis-Poynter, 20 Garrick Street, London WC2E 9BJ

British Copyright Council, 29/33 Berners Street, London W1P 4AA. Tel: 01-930 1911; 01-580 5544

British Library, Copyright Receipt Office, Store Street, London WC1E 7DG. Tel: 01-636 1544

Council for Educational Technology, 3 Devonshire Street, London W1N 2BA. Tel: 01-636 4186

Institute of Information Scientists, Harvest House, 62 London Road, Reading, Berks. RG1 5AJ

Library Association, 7 Ridgmount Street, London WC1E 7AE. Tel: 01-636 7543

Mechanical-Copyright Protection Society Ltd, Elgar House, 380 Streatham High Road, London SW16 6HR. Tel: 01-769 3181

Microfilm Association of Great Britain, 8 High Street, Guildford, Surrey GU2 5AJ. Tel: Godalming (048 68) 6653

Music Publishers Association, 73/75 Mortimer Street, London W1N 7TB

Performing Right Society, 29 Berners Street, London W1. Tel: 01-580 5544

Phonographic Performance Ltd, 62 Oxford Street, London W1. Tel: 01-636 1472

Publishers Association, 19 Bedford Square, London WC1B 3HJ. Tel: 01-580 6321

Royal Society, 6 Carlton House Terrace, London SW1. Tel: 01-839 3561

Society of Authors, 84 Drayton Gardens, London SW10 9SD. Tel: 01-343 0900/6642

Standing Conference of National and University Libraries (SCONUL), 102 Euston Street, London NW1 2HA. Tel: 01-387 0317.

Bibliography

I. British copyright law, commentaries and interpretations

1. Biske, V. 'Some legal aspects of information work' *Aslib proceedings* 10 (2) Feb. 1958 25-37
2. British Copyright Council. *Copying and copyright: are you within the law?* BCC, no date (poster)
   British Copyright Council. *Photocopying and the law* see No. 14.
3. *Copinger and Skone James on copyright*, 11th ed., by E. P. Skone James. Sweet & Maxwell, 1971
4. *Copyright Act, 1956 4 & 5 Eliz. 2 Ch. 74* HMSO, 1956
5. 'Copyright in indexes' *The indexer* 8 (2) Oct. 1972 81-7
6. *The Copyright (Libraries) Regulations 1957* HMSO, 1957 (Statutory Instruments 1957 No. 868)
7. Dain, Neville. 'Librarians and copyright' *Assistant librarian* 50(10) Oct. 1957 169-70
8. Eddy, J. P. *The law of copyright* Butterworths, 1957
9. Garfield, Eugene *and* Sophar, G. 'Is copyright infringement by non-profit organizations always permissible?' *Aslib proceedings* 22 (11) Nov. 1970. 570-1
   replies from D. J. Urquhart, C. W. Cleverdon and G. Woledge in 23 (1) Jan. 1971. 47-50
10. Gibbs-Smith, Charles H. *Copyright law concerning works of art, photographs and the written and spoken word.* 2nd ed. (rev'd). Museums Association, 1974 (Museums Association Information Sheet IS No. 7) first published 1970.
10a. *Copying music : a code of fair practice agreed between composers, publishers and users.* Music Publishers Association, 1979
11. National Council for Educational Technology. Working Group on Rights. *Copyright and education : a guide to the use of copyright material in educational institutions* NCET, 1972 (Working paper No. 8)
    note NCET later became CET (Council for Educational Technology)
12. Pemberton, John E. 'Crown copyright' *Library world* 71 (838) April 1970. 307-8
12a. Ratcliffe, Eric A. 'Notes on copyright, including references to the report of the Whitford Committee.' *Aslib proceedings* 31(7) July 1979. 334-51
13. Science Reference Library. *Photocopy service.* British Library, SRL, 1975 (Aid to readers no. 8)
14. Society of Authors *and* Publishers Association *Photocopying and the law : a guide for librarians and teachers and other suppliers and users of photocopies of copyright works.* S. of A. and P.A., 1965.
    – – – – – 2nd ed., by British Copyright Council, 1970.
15. Staveley, Ronald. *The reader, the writer, and copyright law* University College, London, 1957. (School of Librarianship and Archives Occasional Publications no. 7)

16. Taylor, L. J. *A librarian's handbook*. Library Association, 1976 [1977]
     – – – – – vol. 2. 1980
17. Urquhart, D. J. 'Photocopying and the law of copyright' *Aslib proceedings*
     23 (1) Jan. 1971 47.
     reply to Garfield and Sophar (no. 9 above)
18. Whale, R. F. *Copyright : evolution, theory and practice*. Longman, 1970
19. Woledge, G. 'Copyright and libraries in the United Kingdom' *Journal of
     documentation* 14 (2) June 1958. 45-55
20. Woledge, G. 'Copyright and library photocopying : the practical problems'
     Aslib proceedings 19(7) July 1967. 217-22

II. The reprography debate and the Whitford Report

21. Barker, Ronald E. *Photocopying practices in the United Kingdom*. Faber,
     1970
22. Brophy, Brigid 'Whitford Report' *Bookseller* April 23, 1977. 2172
     reply to a letter from Charles Clark (*Bookseller* April 9, 1977. 2032), which
     he replied to in (with other letters on the subject) *Bookseller* April 20, 1977.
     2262-5.
     Further exchanges in *Bookseller* May 7, 1977. 2354, and May 28, 1977. 2612.
     The subject is 'author's right'.
23. Coleman, Earl. 'The impact of copyright on the future of scholarly publishing'
     Aslib proceedings 29 (7) July 1977 259-65
24. 'Copyright in technical fields : international publishers consider their defences'
     Bookseller November 27, 1976. 2604-6
25. De Freitas, Denis. 'Changing the copyright law' *The author* LXXXV (3)
     Autumn 1974. 104-10
26. Freegard, Michael. 'Collective copyright licensing — surrender or safeguard'
     The author LXXXVI (4) Winter 1974. 141-8
27. 'Gaining ground against copyright erosion (S.T.M. General Assembly)'
     Bookseller November 12, 1977. 2810-11
28. Graham, Gordon. 'Publishers, librarians and photocopying' *Bookseller* Sep-
     tember 24, 1977. 2148-51
29. Kent, A. K. 'Dial-up and die — can information systems survive the on-line
     age?' *Information scientist* 12 (1) March 1978. 3-7
30. Line, Maurice B. *and* Wood, D. N. 'The effect of a large-scale photocopying
     service on journal sales' *Journal of documentation* 31 (4) December 1975.
     234-45
     see also no. 42
31. Line, Maurice B. 'Principles of international lending and photocopying' *Inter-
     national library review* 9, 1977. 369-79
32. New, Peter G. *Reprography for librarians*. Bingley, 1975
33. Oppenheim, C. 'Copyright and scholarly publishing' *Aslib proceedings* 29 (10)
     October 1977. 381-2
     reply to Earl Coleman (no. 23 above)
34. 'Photocopying and breach of copyright' *Bookseller* August 30, 1975. 1444
35. Pinnock, Kenneth. 'Licensing copying' *Bookseller* March 18, 1978. 1893
36. *Report of the Copyright Committee*. HMSO, 1952 (Cmd 8662)
     the Gregory report.
37. 'Revision of interlibrary loan form (ILL) including copyright law representa-
     tions' *Special libraries* November 1977, 415-8
38. Royal Society Information Services Committee. *Fair copying declaration and
     list of publishing organizations subscribing to it*. Royal Society, 1950
     – – – – – 2nd ed. 1952
     – – – – – 3rd ed. 1957
39. Royal Society Scientific Information Conference. *Recommendations adopted
     by the Conference 21 June - 2 July 1948* Royal Society, 1948

40. Samuels, Alex. 'Worth copying, worth protecting: copyright and the university' *New universities quarterly* 31 (1) 1976. 61-72
41. Du Sautoy, Peter. 'Copyright' *Times literary supplement* June 3, 1977. 680
42. Tongeren, E. van. 'The effect of a large-scale photocopying service on journal sales' *Journal of documentation* 32 (3) September, 1976. 198-206
    reply to Line, M. B. and Wood, D. N. no. 30, above, with their rejoinder
43. University of Hull. Brynmor Jones Library. *Coin-operated copiers*. Univ. of Hull, Nov. 1977
44. Weston, Jeremy. 'The unphotocopiable journal' *New scientist* 17 March 1977. 657
45. White, Herbert S. *and* Fry, Bernard M. 'Economic interaction between special libraries and publishers of scholarly and research journals' *Special libraries* March, 1977. 109-14
46. Wood, Kate. 'Copyright 1954-1975: a bibliography' *Library and information bulletin* 23, 1974. 21-38
47. Woodward, A. M. *Factors affecting the renewal of periodical subscriptions: a study of decision-making in libraries with special reference to economics and inter-library lending*. Aslib, 1978.

III. The Whitford Report, evidence and response

48. Aslib. *Aslib's submission to the departmental enquiry on copyright*. 1974
49. British Council. *Memorandum submitted on behalf of the British Council to the departmental committee to consider the law relating to copyright and designs* . . . . [B.C. 1974]. unpublished.
50. *Copyright and designs law: report of the Committee to consider the law on copyright and designs*. HMSO, 1977 (Cmnd 6732)
    the Whitford Report.
51. Council for Educational Technology. *Evidence to the Committee to consider the law on copyright and designs*. CET, [1974] unpublished.
52. Graham, Gordon. 'UK's Whitford Report: faith, hope and clarity' *Publishers weekly* 211(17) 25 Apr. 1977. 49
53. Inner London Education Authority. 'More evidence on copyright' *Bookseller* February 1, 1975. 360-7
    ILEA's evidence to the Whitford Committee reported.
54. Institute of Information Scientists. *Memorandum of evidence to the departmental committee on copyright* [I.I.S.], 1974.
55. The Library Association. *Memorandum of evidence to the departmental committee on copyright*. 1974
    in *A librarian's handbook* vol 1. see no. 16 above
56. The Library Association. *The report of the Whitford Committee: interim statement*. May 1977
    in *A librarian's handbook* vol 2. see no. 16 above
57. MacLeish, Philippa. 'First reactions to Whitford' *The author* LXXXVIII (2) Summer, 1977. 58-62
58. 'P.A. Submission on Whitford report' *Bookseller* March 18, 1978 1896-9
59. 'Photocopying and fair dealing: submissions to the departmental committee' *Bookseller* September 7, 1974. 1728
    submissions by British Copyright Council and British Printing Industries Federation summarised
60. Publishers Association. *Submission to the Whitford Committee appointed to consider the law on copyright and designs* P.A., 1974. unpublished
61. Royal Society. *Comments on the report of the Whitford Committee on copyright and designs law*. Royal Society, 1978 (Press Release PR/4(78))
62. Standing Conference of National and University Libraries. *Submission to the Whitford inquiry on copyright*. SCONUL, 1974 (SCONUL C Doc 74/56 Rev. 1 R)
63. Taylor, L. J. 'Copyright and the Whitford Report' *in Proceedings of the 25th*

annual study group, Sheffield, April 15th - 18th, 1977. Library Association, RSIS, 1977. p. 5-23

64. University of London. Library Resources Co-ordinating Committee. *Response to the Report of the Committee to consider the law on copyright and designs 1977.* Univ. of London, LRCC, 1977 (Appendix LRCC November 1977). in *A librarian's handbook* vol 2. see no. 16 above

65. [Walter, R. M.]. 'Whitford calls for blanket licensing of copyright — an example for PLR?' *Library Association record* 79 (4) April 1977. 172

66. 'The Whitford Report on copyright I' *Bookseller* March 26, 1977. 1842-5
----- II *Bookseller* April 2, 1977. 1943-9

IV. Copyright and education

67. 'Copying in schools: P.A. offers draft license as basis for discussion' *Bookseller* October 25, 1975. 2180-7

68. *Copyright: an 'Education' digest* Education (periodical) 19 October, 1973. an insert also published separately

69. Council for Educational Technology. *Conference on copyright, 21st March 1974: summary.* CET, [1974].

70. Council for Educational Technology. *Negotiating arrangements for educational copying following the Whitford Report.* [CET, 1977]

71. Council for Educational Technology *and* Publishers Association *Report of a survey of the copying of print materials by schools* P.A., 1975

72. Crabb, Geoffrey. *Copyright and contract: a course workbook.* CET, 1976

73. Crabb, Geoffrey. 'Copyright in the AV library' *Audio visual librarian* 2(4) Spring 1976. 153-7

74. Golub, Melinda V. 'Not by books alone: library copying of non-print, copyrighted material' *Law library journal* 70(2) May 1977. 153-70

75. Griffin, Penny. 'How copyright puts shackles on the teaching of drama' *Times educational supplement* 18 November, 1977. 13

76. Hughes, Noel. 'Brains for the picking' *Times educational supplement* 11th March, 1977. 3.

77. McNally, Paul T. 'Non-book materials and copyright' *Australian library journal* Nov. 1978. 314-23

78. Richardson, Paul. 'Copying and copyright in schools: a personal view' *Bookseller.* February 7, 1976. 422-30

V. Special aspects of copyright

79. 'ADAPSO urges stronger copyright laws for computer programs and software' *Information hotline* Jan. 1978. 1, 7-8

80. Bell, 'Legal deposit in Britain (Part 1)' *Law librarian* 1977. 5-8
----- (Part 2) 8(2) August 1977. 22-6

81. CRC Systems Incorporated. 'Impact of information technology on copyright law in the use of computerized scientific and technological information systems' *in* Technology and copyright p. 137-204. see no. 133

82. 'CONTU interprets new copyright law as shelter for computer programs. . .' *Information hotline* 9 (8) September 1977 1, 10-12

83. Dreyfus, John. 'Type design: the rationale for copyright protection' *Publishers weekly* January 6, 1975. 42-6
(extract from a 1974 seminar paper by a British typographer)

84. Henderson, Madeline M. 'Copyright impacts of future technology' *Journal of chemical information and computer science* 16 1976. 72-4

85. Hersey, John 'Dissent from CONTU's software recommendation' reprinted from Final Report of CONTU, in *Technology and copyright* p.247-63. see no. 133

86. Johnston, Dan. *Design protection: a guide to the law on plagiarism for manufacturers and designers* Design Council, 1978
87. Linden, Bella L. 'Copyright, photocopying, and computer usage' *Bulletin of the American Society for Information Science* 1 (10) May, 1975. 12-14
88. Microfilm Association of Great Britain 'Submissions to the Whitford Committee on copyright' *Microdoc* 13 (4), 1974 113-17
89. Osborne, Chris. *A copyright clearance exercise (1976-1978)* Middlesex Polytechnic, 1978
90. Powell, David J. 'The law of copyright in relation to publications on microfilm' *Microdoc* 13 (2), 1974. 34-7
91. Squires, Jeffrey. 'Copyright and compilations in the computer era: old wine in new bottles' *Bulletin of the Copyright Society of the USA* 24, October 1976. 18-46
    and in *Technology and copyright* p. 205-33 see no. 133
91a. Tapper, Colin. *Computer law*. Longman, 1978.

VI. The United States copyright revision and the new law

92. American Library Association. 'Librarian's guide to the new copyright law' *Bowker annual . . . .* 1977. 117-58
93. *Bowker annual of library and book trade information* 22nd ed. 1977, ed. N. B. Glick and S. L. Prakken. R. R. Bowker, 1977 includes brief highlights of new copyright law; ALA's Librarian's guide to new copyright law; articles by J. J. Marke and Charles H. Lieb, and complete text of new law PL 94-553
94. Butler, Meredith. 'Copyright and reserve books — what libraries are doing' *College and research libraries news* 39 (3) May, 1978. 125-30
95. Copyright Clearance Center, Inc. *Handbook for libraries and other organizational users which copy from serials and separates* CCC, October, 1977
96. 'Copyright revision' *Special libraries* July, 1976. 327-35
    (statements from 6 library associations to the House Committee on revision of the Copyright Bill)
97. 'Copyright — the new US law' *New scientist* 12 January, 1978. 110
98. *Information hotline* special copyright issue. 8 (10) November, 1976.
    (includes full text of new copyright law; report by House and Senate Joint Committee on copyright revision; Guidelines for classroom copying . . . , CONTU guidelines on library photocopying; and article 'Copyright in the 1980's', by Barbara Ringer see no. 128)
99. Johnston, Donald F. *Copyright handbook*. R. R. Bowker, 1978
100. Lieb, Charles H. 'An overview of the new copyright law' in *Bowker annual . . . .* 1977. 164-71
101. Marke, Julius J. 'Copyright revision and issues of continuing concern to the librarian' *Bowker annual . . . .* 1977. 159-63
102. Marke, Julius J. 'Copyright revision in the United States of America' *International j. of law librarianship* 5. March 1977. 121-30
103. Marke, Julius J. 'United States copyright revision and its legislative history' *Law library journal* 70 (2) May, 1977. 121-52
104. Martell, Charles. 'Copyright law and reserve operations — an interpretation' *College and research libraries news* 39 (1) Jan. 1978. 1-6
105. Miller, Jerome K. *Applying the new copyright law: a guide for educators and librarians* American Library Association, 1979
106. 'The new copyright law: final regulation: warning of copyright for use by libraries and archives' *Information hotline* Jan. 1978. 15-16
    excerpted from *Federal register* Wed. 16 Nov. 1977 59264-5
107. *The new copyright law: questions teachers and librarians ask* National Education Association, 1977.
108. 'New rules on photocopy limits and classroom use set forth in full text of copyright addenda' *American libraries* November, 1976. 610-11

109. Peters, Marybeth. 'New copyright law: developments and issues in the first
     year of operation' *Bowker annual* . . . . 24th ed. 1979 42-6
110. Ringer, Barbara. 'Copyright in the 1980's' *Information hotline* 8 (10)
     November 1976. 28-31
     6th Donald C. Brace Memorial Lecture, March 25, 1976
111. Ringer, Barbara. 'Finding your way around in the new copyright law'
     Publishers weekly December 13, 1976. 38-41
112. Thatcher, Sanford. 'A publisher's guide to the new U.S. copyright law'
     Scholarly publishing July, 1977. 315-33
113. U.S. Library of Congress. Copyright Office. *Reproduction of copyrighted
     works by educators and librarians.* L.C., 1978 (Circular R21)
114. Wagner, Susan. 'Lawyers warn publishers: copyright countdown has begun'
     Publishers weekly March 7, 1977. 56-8
115. Wagner, Susan. 'New copyright law primer Part 1: the basics' *Publishers
     weekly* December 26, 1977. 37-42
     – – – – 'Part 2 the formalities' 213(5) 30 Jan. 1978. 65-70
116. Wagner, Susan. 'The new US copyright law' *The author* LXXXVII (4)
     Winter 1976. 125-9
117. Wagner, Susan 'S22 copyrighted 1976: Congress approves "monumental
     bill" ' *Publishers weekly* October 11, 1976. 22-24
     – – – – – continued as 'Copying and the copyright bill: where the new revision
     stands on "fair use" ' *Publishers weekly*, October 18, 1976. 28-30
118. *Washington newsletter* 28 (13) November 13, 1976. special issue on new
     copyright law.
     contains librarian's guide to new copyright law, excerpts from the law, and
     three sets of guidelines, with excerpts from Congressional reports.

VII. The United States reprographic debate

119. Clapp, Verner W. 'Libraries — on the spot with present and future legislation'
     in *Copyright — the librarian and the law*, ed. G. J. Lukac, Rutgers Univ.,
     Graduate School of Library Service, 1972. 59-71
120. De Gennaro, Richard. 'Copyright, resource sharing, and hard times: a view
     from the field' *American libraries* 8 (9) September 1977. 430-5
     and in *Technology and copyright* p. 399-414 see no. 132
121. Fry, Bernard M. and White, Herbert S. *Publishers and libraries: a study of
     scholarly and research journals* Lexington books, 1976
122. 'High Court deadlock affirms photocopying okay' *Library journal* April 1,
     1975. 619-20
123. King Research Inc. *Library photocopying in the United States: with impli-
     cations for the development of a copyright royalty payment mechanism* . . . .
     National Commission on Libraries and Information Science, 1977
124. Nasri, William Z. *Crisis in copyright* Marcel Dekker, 1976
125. National Commission on New Technological Uses of Copyrighted Works
     (CONTU). *Meeting (9th) held at Arlington, Va. on October 21, 1976.* US
     Dept. of Commerce, NTIS, 1976 (PB 261947)
126. National Commission on New Technological Uses of Copyrighted Works
     (CONTU) *Preliminary report, October 8, 1976.* CONTU, 1976
127. 'Proposals solicited for design and operation of "Copyright Clearance Center"
     for copyrighted works' *Information hotline* 9 (8) September 1977, 1, 12-15
128. Ringer, Barbara. 'The demonology of copyright' *Publishers weekly* November
     18, 1974. 26-30
129. Risher, Carol. 'The National Commission on New Technological Uses of
     Copyrighted Works (CONTU)' *Serials librarian* 2 (2) Winter, 1977. 129-37
130. Special Libraries Association. 'Copyright and NTIS' *Special libraries*
     December, 1976. 591-2
131. Stevenson, Iris Caroline. 'The doctrine of fair use as it affects libraries' *Law
     library journal* 68 (3) Aug. 1975. 254-73

132. *Technology and copyright: sources and materials*, ed. George P. Bush and Robert H. Dreyfuss, rev'd ed. Lomond Publications, 1979. Part I Annotated bibliography p. 1-118; Part II Selected materials p. 119-533 (19 articles etc.); Indexes etc. p. 534-552

133. Thatcher, Sanford G. 'On fair use and library photocopying' *Scholarly publishing* July, 1978. 313-34

134. Wagner, Susan. 'Supreme Court ruling fails to resolve photocopying issues' *Publishers weekly* 207 (22) March 10, 1975. 75

135. Whitestone, Patricia. 'Paying for copying in the U.S.A.' *Bookseller* August 20, 1977. 1570-1

136. *The Williams and Wilkins case: the Williams and Wilkins Company v. the United States* v.1. comp. Marilyn G. McCormick. Science Associates/International Inc., and Mansell Information/Publishing Ltd, 1974. no more published.

137. Wood, D. N. 'Photocopying in the United States' *Interlending review* 6 (2) April 1978. 66-9

VIII. Copyright in Europe and the Commonwealth

138. Benjamin, Curtis G. 'Regulation of photocopying: a world-wide quandary' *Library journal* September 1, 1975. 1481-3

139. Catterns, D. 'Librarians and the law of copyright' *Australian library journal* November, 1973. 408-15

140. Dietz, Adolf. *Copyright law in the European Community: a comparative investigation of national copyright legislation, with special reference to the provisions of the Treaty establishing the European Economic Community* Sijthoff & Noordhoff, 1978

141. Fabinyi, Andrew. 'The Franki report and reprographic reproduction' *Australian academic and research libraries* March, 1977. 1-3

142. Ferguson, G. A. 'Photocopying: an Australian view of the problem' *Scholarly publishing* October, 1976. 23-34

143. Gillespie, Paul D. *and others. Problems of document delivery for the Euronet user* (final report), prepared for the Commission of the European Communities, Directorate General for Scientific and Technical Information and Information Management. Franklin Institute GmbH, October 1978. various paging.

144. Hall, James. 'Little comfort for publishers in Franki report' *Bookseller* 5 February, 1977. 420-4

145. Horton, Allan. 'After the Franki report — what ?' *Australian academic and research libraries* March 1977. 4-8

146. Lottman, Herbert R. 'Photocopying: how is Europe handling the problem ?' *Publishers weekly* November 25, 1974. 26-7

147. Menzinger, Klaus. 'Copyright and photocopying: revision debates in the Federal Republic of Germany' *Interlending review* 8 (1) 1980. 20-3 paper given to Plenary Session of IFLA 45th Council at Copenhagen August 1979.

148. 'The New South Wales judgment' *Bookseller* September 7, 1974. 1732-4

149. Pearce, Dennis. 'Librarians and copyright: great expectations' *Australian library journal* February 1977. 14-17

150. Pearce, D. C. 'Photocopying and copyright' *Australian library journal* February, 1973. 5-17

151. *Report of the Copyright Law Committee on Reprographic Reproduction October, 1976*. Canberra, Australian Government Publishing Service, 1976. the Franki report

152. Keyes, A. A. 'Copyright revision in Canada' *Canadian library journal* 34 (5) October 1977. 401-7

153. McQueen, David. 'Copyright' *Canadian library journal* 32 (6) December 1975. 433-49

154.   White, Harold T. 'Photocopying — the new treason?' *New Zealand libraries*
        40 (1) Spring 1977. 31-3
155.   Wylie, D. M. 'Photocopying — the new heresy?' *New Zealand libraries* 39
        (5) October, 1976. 174-88
156.   Zaaiman, R. B. 'Copyright and its implications for reprography' *South
        African libraries* 44 (4) April, 1977. 139-52.

Index

References are not to page numbers, but to paragraph numbers, and where necessary, subsections of paragraphs.
Abbreviations used:

ALPSP   Association of Learned and Professional Society Publishers
BC   British Council
BCC   British Copyright Council
BLLD   British Library Lending Division
BPIF   British Printing Industries Federation
CET   Council for Educational Technology
IIS   Institute of Information Scientists
ILEA   Inner London Education Authority
LA   Library Association
MAGB   Microfilm Association of Great Britain
PA   Publishers Association
PLR   Public Lending Right
RS   Royal Society
SA   Society of Authors
SCONUL Standing Conference of National and University Libraries
UL   University of London
US   United States

A LIBRARIAN'S HANDBOOK
by L. J. Taylor 2 vols. 1977-80

*contains, among hundreds of other useful documents, several texts
on copyright, referred to in this book:*

v.1
Copyright Act 1956 (excerpts)
Copyright (Libraries) Regulations 1957
Copyright Act 1911 (excerpt)
LA evidence to Whitford Committee

v.2
Whitford Report (excerpts)
comments on the report by the LA, SCONUL,
    University of London, Royal Society, and CET
US Copyright Law 1976 (excerpts) and CONTU
    Guidelines (complete)
Ordnance Survey Copyright regulations for libraries
Unesco Guidelines for copyright information centres

The Library Association, 7 Ridgmount Street,
London, WC1E 7AE
vol. 1 £15 (£12 to members)
vol. 2 £25 (£20 to members)